Our Country

Our Country

Classic Australian Poetry

*From the Colonial Ballads
to Paterson & Lawson*

*Edited
by
Michael Cook*

LITTLE HILLS PRESS

©Little Hills Press 2007

Our Country
ISBN 1 86315 2326

Edited by Michael Cook
Layout and design by Michael Brown
Cover design by Michael Brown

Printed in China through Colorcraft Ltd, Hong Kong.

Published by Little Hills Press
Unit 12, 103 Kurrajong Avenue
Mount Druitt NSW 2770 Australia

lhills@bigpond.net.au
www.littlehills.com

All rights reserved. No part of this publication may be
reproduced, stored in a retrieval system, or transmitted
in any form or by any means, electronic, mechanical,
photocopying, recording or otherwise, without the prior
permission in writing of the publisher.

Little Hills™ Press and  are trademarks of
Little Hills Press Pty Ltd

Contents

Introduction 9

Bush Yarns

The Sick Stockrider – ***Adam Lindsay Gordon***	14
The Great Australian Adjective – ***W.T. Goodge***	17
McCarthy's Brew: A Gulf Country Yarn – ***George Essex Evans***	18
Who's Riding Old Harlequin Now? ***Harry ('Breaker') Morant***	20
The Geebung Polo Club – ***A.B. ('Banjo') Paterson***	23
Mulga Bill's Bicycle – ***A.B. ('Banjo') Paterson***	25
A Bush Christening – ***A.B. ('Banjo') Paterson***	27
The Man from Snowy River – ***A.B. ('Banjo') Paterson***	29
Said Hanrahan – ***P.J. Hartigan (John O'Brien)***	33

The Golden Past

Clancy of the Overflow – ***A.B. ('Banjo') Paterson***	38
Old Australian Ways – ***A.B. ('Banjo') Paterson***	40
The Song of Old Joe Swallow – ***Henry Lawson***	43
They've Builded... – ***Furnley Maurice (Frank Wilmot)***	46
Echoes of Wheels... – ***Furnley Maurice (Frank Wilmot)***	47
Return – ***'E' (Mary Fullerton)***	49

Colonial Ballads

Jim Jones at Botany Bay – ***Anon.***	52
A Convict's Lament on the Death of Captain Logan – ***Anon.***	53
Colonial Experience – ***Anon.***	55
Botany Bay Courtship – ***Anon.***	57
The Wild Colonial Boy – ***Anon.***	59
The Maranoa Drivers – ***Anon.***	61
The Diggins-Oh – ***Anon.***	62

New Landscapes

The Kangaroo – *Barron Field*	66
A Hot Day in Sydney – *Anon.*	68
The Beautiful Land of Australia – *Anon.*	72
Where the Pelican Builds – *Mary Hannay Foott*	75
The Song of the Shingle-Splitters – *Henry Kendall*	76
Bell-Birds – *Henry Kendall*	78
Dawn and Sunrise in the Snowy Mountains – *Charles Harpur*	80
A Midsummer Noon in the Australian Forest – *Charles Harpur*	81
The West Coasters (Tasmania) – *Marie E.J. Pitt*	83
A Gallop of Fire – *Marie E.J. Pitt*	85
On the Derwent – *Frank Penn-Smith*	86
The Poor, Poor Country – *John Shaw Neilson*	87
My Country – *Dorothea Mackellar*	89
The Banksia – *Wolfe Fairbridge*	91

Personal Visions

The Banks of the Condamine – *Anon.*	94
Emus – *'E' (Mary Fullerton)*	96
Because she would ask me why I loved her – *Christopher John Brennan*	97
A gray and dusty daylight flows – *Christopher John Brennan*	98
Fire in the Heavens – *Christopher John Brennan*	99
The Smoker Parrot – *John Shaw Neilson*	100
Song Be Delicate – *John Shaw Neilson*	101
Native Companions Dancing – *John Shaw Neilson*	102
The Orange Tree – *John Shaw Neilson*	103

Battlers

Christmas Day near Lake Torrens, 1864 – *Robert Bruce*	106
Where the Dead Men Lie – *Barcroft Boake*	109
Jim's Whip – *Barcroft Boake*	111
The Shearer's Wife – *Louis Esson*	113
The Women of the West – *George Essex Evans*	114
Middleton's Rouseabout – *Henry Lawson*	116
Past Carin' – *Henry Lawson*	117
Since the Country Carried Sheep – *Harry ('Breaker') Morant*	119
Butchered To Make a Dutchman's Holiday – *Harry ('Breaker') Morant*	121
The Trenches – *Frederic Manning*	123
11.11.1918 – *J.A.R. McKellar*	125

City Life

The Man from Ironbark – *A.B. ('Banjo') Paterson*	128
The Call of Stoush – *C.J. Dennis*	130
Washing Day – *C.J. Dennis*	134
At the Play – *C.J. Dennis*	137
The Woman at the Washtub – *Victor Daley*	141
The Yellow Gas – *Christopher John Brennan*	143
Football Field: Evening – *J.A.R. McKellar*	145

Politics

Song of the Squatter – *Robert Lowe*	148
The Last Of His Tribe – *Henry Kendall*	150
Are You the Cove? – *Joseph Furphy (Tom Collins)*	152
Second-Class Wait Here – *Henry Lawson*	153
Freedom on the Wallaby – *Henry Lawson*	155
Faces in the Street – *Henry Lawson*	157
Waltzing Matilda – *A.B. ('Banjo') Paterson*	161
Tall Hat – *Victor Daley*	163

The Glorious Future

from 'Australasia' - **William Charles Wentworth**	166
Colonial Nomenclature - **John Dunmore Lang**	168
The Australian Sunrise - **James Cuthbertson**	170
Our Coming Countrymen - **Henry Parkes**	171
The Australian - **Arthur Henry Adams**	174
The Song of Australia - **Caroline Carleton**	177

Index

Titles and authors	180
First lines	185
Acknowledgements	189

Introduction

To its early European settlers, Australia hardly seemed suited for poetical effusion. Colonial society was overshadowed by the presence of thousands of convicts and preoccupied with the toil of conquering and administering the new land. The landscape was hot, harsh and arid. The infant colony was maturing at the same time as the Romantic poets, especially William Wordsworth, were transforming English poetry, but the bleak Australian bush resisted translation into the sublime and uplifting sentiments of conventional Romantic verse.

Some of the Nineteenth Century poems in this volume show how inadequate early Australian poets felt in a land which they were the first to describe in English. The Aborigines had their own poetic traditions, but these were a closed book to the new-comers. Banjo Paterson's 1905 anthology *Old Bush Songs*, included two Aboriginal songs in an unidentified language with a pathetic note from a contributor: "I could never find out what the words meant, and I don't think the blacks themselves knew." It was only in the Twentieth Century that English-speaking Australian poets were able to tap into the songs and epics of their ancient continent, thanks to the efforts of anthropologists.

So, to the colonials, Australian landscapes, flora and fauna were often regarded as ghastly and weird — not enchanting and sublime, as they ought to be, according to Romantic conventions. Barron Field was the author of the first book of verse to be printed in New South Wales, *First Fruits of Australian Poetry*. Unsurprisingly, he was perplexed. "New South Wales is a perpetual flower-garden, but there is not a single scene in it of which a painter could make a landscape," he wrote for readers back home in England.

It is with this sense of inadequacy in mind that the more ambitious sort of poetry written in the Nineteenth Century should be read. The achievement of Charles Harpur and Henry Kendall, who were probably the most technically accomplished poets of the colonial period, was their attempt to use the language of European Romanticism to create poetry fit for a new world. How successful they were can only be appreciated by reading the awkward and banal warblings of their deservedly forgotten contemporaries.

On the other hand, the ballad tradition flourished in colonial Australia. The convicts, the early settlers and the diggers on the goldfields were familiar with popular English and Irish ballads and adapted them to their new environment, chronicling its hardships, politics and adventures. These examples seldom attain the pathos and poignancy of the Scottish border ballads. Nonetheless, many of the ballads have a vigour and freshness whose appeal has survived Australia's transformation from a rough-hewn, agricultural colony into a sophisticated, post-industrial, multi cultural federation.

The authors of many of the ballads were anonymous, but in the closing years of the Nineteenth Century, several "bush poets" emerged who combined fluency in verse with experience of life on the land. Their writing helped to transform "the Bush" from a term of geography into a resonant symbol of the new nation. They wrote about tough and inexpressive battlers who lived lives of quiet nobility and heroism. Early writers in this vein were Adam Lindsay Gordon, Barcroft Boake and "Breaker" Morant. The first two committed suicide and the third was shot for war crimes during the Boer War — a sombre reflection of the dour battle which life in the Bush represented for many people.

The two great names in the ballad tradition are Henry Lawson and A.B. "Banjo" Paterson. Like many of his better short stories, Lawson's poems are often hard-edged social criticism depicting battlers with compassion and their oppressors with scorn. The poems of Paterson, however, glow with a sunny innocence, combining heroism and endurance with playful optimism. Paterson did not have an original, inquiring mind, but he shaped the Australian self-image as few other writers have.

Introduction

The turn of the century also brought a wider range of theme, more sophisticated versification and more engagement with poetry in England and other European cultures. The most impressive of these figures was Christopher Brennan, a scholar of classics and German who wrote mysteriously beautiful verse which often demands academic commentary to be understood. Australian culture acquires a new dimension when one reflects that Brennan, who was heavily influenced by French Symbolist poets and German philosophers, was writing at the same time as the Bulletin was promoting bush poetry as our national idiom.

Almost miraculously, one poet was both "classic Aussie battler" in the line of Lawson and Paterson and a delicate, complex, graceful lyricist like Brennan: John Shaw Neilson. For much of his life, Neilson was an itinerant labourer who cleared land, picked fruit, dug in quarries and built fences. His eyes were so bad that he could only read large print. Despite these obstacles, he composed some of the most musical, subtle and tender poems ever published in Australia. Too little read, Neilson is one of the great figures of our literature.

World War I was a landmark for Australian verse. Although there were no great Australian war poets, as there were in England, the national mood changed and the poetry changed with it. Poets became more in touch with international influences, more personal, more self-critical and less concerned with celebrating the victories and hardships of life in the bush. Figures like Furnley Maurice, Mary Fullerton and J.A.R. McKellar wrote poems which are distinctively Twentieth Century in their interpretation of Australian life.

What we have tried to show in this selection of early Australian verse, ranging from convict days to the classic voices of Henry Lawson and "Banjo" Paterson, to the first glimmerings of modern verse, is the great variety of our poetic heritage. In a short hundred or so years, English-speaking migrants settled a new land, came to terms with it and began to love it. We should be proud of this legacy.

Michael Cook

Bush Yarns

Bush Yarns

The Sick Stockrider
Adam Lindsay Gordon (1833 - 1870)

Hold hard, Ned! Lift me down once more, and lay me in
        the shade.
    Old man, you've had your work cut out to guide
Both horses, and to hold me in the saddle when I sway'd,
    All through the hot, slow, sleepy, silent ride.
The dawn at "Moorabinda" was a mist rack dull and dense,
    The sunrise was a sullen, sluggish lamp;
I was dozing in the gateway at Arbuthnot's bound'ry fence,
    I was dreaming on the Limestone cattle camp.
We crossed the creek at Carricksford, and sharply through
        the haze,
    And suddenly the sun shot flaming forth;
To southward lay "Katâwa", with the sandpeaks all ablaze,
    And the flush'd fields of Glen Lomond lay to north.
Now westward winds the bridle path that leads to Lindisfarm,
    And yonder looms the double-headed Bluff;
From the far side of the first hill, when the skies are clear
        and calm,
    You can see Sylvester's woolshed fair enough.
Five miles we used to call it from our homestead to the place
    Where the big tree spans the roadway like an arch;
'Twas here we ran the dingo down that gave us such a chase
    Eight years ago — or was it nine? — last March.

'Twas merry in the glowing morn, among the gleaming grass,
    To wander as we've wandered many a mile,
And blow the cool tobacco cloud, and watch the white
        wreaths pass,
    Sitting loosely in the saddle all the while.
'Twas merry 'mid the blackwoods, when we spied the
        station roofs,
    To wheel the wild scrub cattle at the yard,
With a running fire of stockwhips and a fiery run of hoofs;
    Oh! the hardest day was never then too hard!

The Sick Stockrider

Aye! we had a glorious gallop after "Starlight" and his gang,
    When they bolted from Sylvester's on the flat;
How the sun-dried reed-beds crackled, how the flint-strewn
        ranges rang
    To the strokes of "Mountaineer" and "Acrobat".
Hard behind them in the timber, harder still across the heath,
    Close beside them through the tea-tree scrub we dash'd;
And the golden-tinted fern leaves, how they rustled underneath!
    And the honeysuckle osiers, how they crash'd!

We led the hunt throughout, Ned, on the chestnut and the grey,
    And the troopers were three hundred yards behind,
While we emptied our six-shooters on the bushrangers at bay,
    In the creek with stunted box-tree for a blind!
There you grappled with the leader, man to man and horse
        to horse,
    And you roll'd together when the chestnut rear'd;
He blazed away and missed you in that shallow watercourse —
    A narrow shave — his powder singed your beard!
In these hours when life is ebbing, how those days when life
        was young
    Come back to us; how clearly I recall
Even the yarns Jack Hall invented, and the songs Jem Roper
        sung;
    And where are now Jem Roper and Jack Hall?
Aye! nearly all our comrades of the old colonial school,
    Our ancient boon companions, Ned, are gone;
Hard livers for the most part, somewhat reckless as a rule,
    It seems that you and I are left alone.

There was Hughes, who got in trouble through that business
        with the cards,
    It matters little what became of him;
But a steer ripp'd up MacPherson in the Cooraminta yards,
    And Sullivan was drown'd at Sink-or-swim.

Bush Yarns

And Mostyn — poor Frank Mostyn — died at last a fearful wreck,
    In "the horrors", at the Upper Wandinong,
And Carisbrooke, the rider, at the Horsefall broke his neck,
    Faith! the wonder was he saved his neck so long!
Ah! those days and nights we squandered at the Logans' in
        the glen —
    The Logans, man and wife, have long been dead.
Elsie's tallest girl seems taller than your little Elsie then;
    And Ethel is a woman grown and wed.

I've had my share of pastime, and I've done my share of toil,
    And life is short — the longest life a span;
I care not now to tarry for the corn or for the oil,
    Or for the wine that maketh glad the heart of man.
For good undone and gifts misspent and resolutions vain,
    'Tis somewhat late to trouble. This I know —
I should live the same life over, if I had to live again;
    And the chances are I go where most men go.

The deep blue skies wax dusky, and the tall green trees
        grow dim,
    The sward beneath me seems to heave and fall;
And sickly, smoky shadows through the sleepy sunlight swim,
    And on the very sun's face weave their pall.
Let me slumber in the hollow where the wattle blossoms wave,
    With never stone or rail to fence my bed;
Should the sturdy station children pull the bush flowers on
        my grave,
    I may chance to hear them romping overhead.

The Great Australian Adjective

W.T. Goodge (1862 - 1909)

The sunburnt —— stockman stood
And, in a dismal —— mood,
Apostrophized his —— cuddy;
"The —— nag's no —— good,
He couldn't earn his —— food —
A regular —— brumby,
 ——!"

He jumped across the —— horse
And cantered off, of —— course!
The roads were bad and —— muddy;
Said he, "Well, spare me —— days
The —— Government's —— ways
Are screamin' —— funny,
 ——!"

He rode up hill, down —— dale,
The wind it blew a —— gale,
The creek was high and —— floody.
Said he, "The —— horse must swim,
The same for —— me and him,
Is something —— sickenin',
 ——!"

He plunged into the —— creek,
The —— horse was —— weak,
The stockman's face a —— study!
And though the —— horse was drowned
The —— rider reached the ground
Ejaculating, "——?"
 ——!"

17

Bush Yarns

McCarthy's Brew: A Gulf Country Yarn

George Essex Evans (1863 - 1909)

The teams of Black McCarthy crawled adown the Norman Road,
The ground was bare, the bullocks spare, and grievous
    was the load,
And the brown hawks wheeled above them and the heat-waves
    throbbed and glowed.

With lolling tongues and blood-shot eyes and sinews all a-strain
McCarthy's bullocks staggered on across the sun-cracked plain,
The wagon's lumbering after and the drivers raising Cain...

Three mournful figures sat around the camp-fire's fitful glare —
McKinlay Jim and "Spotty" and McCarthy's self they were —
But their spirits were so dismal that they couldn't raise a swear!

'Twas not the long, dry stage ahead that made those bold hearts
    shrink,
The drought-cursed ground, the dying stock, the water thick
    as ink,
But — the drinking curse was on them, and they had no grog
    to drink!

Then with a bound up from the ground, McCarthy jumped
    and cried:
"'Tis vain! 'Tis vain! I go insane. These pangs in my inside!
Some sort of grog, for love of God, invent, concoct, provide!"

McKinlay Jim straight answered him: "Those lotions, sauce,
    and things
Should surely make a brew to slake these thirst sufferings —
A brew that slakes, a brew that wakes and burns and bucks
    and stings."

McCarthy's Brew: A Gulf Country Yarn

Down came the cases from the load — they wrenched them
    wide with force.
They poured and mixed and stirred a brew that would have
    killed a horse —
Cayenne, pain-killer, pickles, embrocation, Worcester sauce!

O, wild and high and fierce and free the orgy rose that night;
The songs they sang, the deeds they did, no poet could indite;
To see them pass that billy round — it was a fearsome sight.

The dingo heard them and with tail between his legs he fled!
The curlew saw them and he ceased his wailing for the dead!
Each frightened bullock on the plain went straightway off
    his head!

Alas! and there are those who say that at the dawn of day
Three perforated carriers round a smoking camp-fire lay:
They did not think McCarthy's brew would take them in
    that way!

McCarthy's teams at Normanton no more the Gulf men see.
McCarthy's bullocks roam the wilds exuberant and free;
McCarthy lies — an instance of preserved anatomee!

Go. Take the moral of this song, which in deep grief I write:
Don't ever drink McCarthy's brew. Be warned in case you might —
Gulf whisky kills at twenty yards, but this stuff kills at sight!

Bush Yarns

Who's Riding Old Harlequin Now?

Harry "Breaker" Morant (1864 - 1902)

They are mustering cattle on Brigalow Vale
    Where the stock-horses whinny and stamp,
And where long Andy Ferguson, you may go bail,
    Is yet boss on a cutting-out camp.
Half the duffers I met would not know a fat steer
    From a blessed old Alderney cow.
Whilst they're mustering there I am wondering here —
    Who is riding brown Harlequin now?

Are the pikers as wild and the scrubs just as dense
    In the brigalow country as when
There was never a homestead and never a fence
    Between Brigalow Vale and The Glen?
Do they yard the big micks 'neath the light of the moon?
    Do the yard-wings re-echo the row
Of stockwhips and hoof-beats? And what sort of coon
    Is there riding old Harlequin now?

There was buckjumping blood in the brown gelding's veins,
    But, lean-headed, with iron-like pins,
Of Pyrrhus and Panic he'd plentiful strains,
    All their virtues, and some of their sins.
'Twas pity, some said, that so shapely a colt
    Fate should with such temper endow;
He would kick and would strike, he would buck and would bolt —
    Ah! who's riding brown Harlequin now?

Who's Riding Old Harlequin Now?

A demon to handle! a devil to ride!
    Small wonder the surcingle burst;
You'd have thought that he'd buck himself out of his hide
    On the morning we saddled him first.
I can mind how he cow-kicked the spur on my boot,
    And though that's long ago, still I vow
If they're wheeling a piker no new-chum galoot
    Is a-riding old Harlequin now!

I remember the boss — how he chuckled and laughed
    When they yarded the brown colt for me:
"He'll be steady enough when we finish the graft
    And have cleaned up the scrubs of Glen Leigh!'
I am wondering today if the brown horse yet live,
    For the fellow who broke him, I trow,
A long lease of soul-ease would willingly give
    To be riding brown Harlequin now!

"Do you think you can hold him?" old Ferguson said —
    He was mounted on Hornet, the grey;
I think Harlequin heard him — he shook his lean head,
    And he needed no holding that day.
Not a prick from a spur, nor a sting from a whip
    As he raced among deadwood and bough
While I sat fairly quiet and just let him rip —
    But who's riding old Harlequin now?

Bush Yarns

I could hear 'em a-crashing the gidgee in front
    As the Bryan colt streaked to the lead
Whilst the boss and the niggers were out of the hunt.
    For their horses lacked Harlequin's speed;
The pikers were yarded and skies growing dim
    When old Fergie was fain to allow:
"The colt's track through the scrub was a knocker" to him —
    But who's riding brown Harlequin now?

From starlight to starlight — all day in between
    The foam-flakes might fly from his bit,
But whatever the pace of the day's work had been,
    The brown gelding was eager and fit.
On the packhorse's back they are fixing a load
    Where the path climbs the hill's gloomy brow;
They are mustering bullocks to send on the road,
    But — who's riding old Harlequin now?

The Geebung Polo Club

A.B. "Banjo" Paterson (1864 - 1941)

It was somewhere up the country in a land of rock and scrub,
That they formed an institution called the Geebung Polo Club.
They were long and wiry natives of the rugged mountainside,
And the horse was never saddled that the Geebungs couldn't ride;
But their style of playing polo was irregular and rash —
They had mighty little science, but a mighty lot of dash:
And they played on mountain ponies that were muscular
    and strong,
Though their coats were quite unpolished, and their manes and
    tails were long.
And they used to train those ponies wheeling cattle in the scrub:
They were demons, were the members of the Geebung
    Polo Club.

It was somewhere down the country, in a city's smoke and
    steam,
That a polo club existed, called the Cuff and Collar Team.
As a social institution 'twas a marvellous success,
For the members were distinguished by exclusiveness and dress.
They had natty little ponies that were nice, and smooth, and
    sleek,
For their cultivated owners only rode 'em once a week.
So they started up the country in pursuit of sport and fame,
For they meant to show the Geebungs how they ought to play
    the game;
And they took their valets with them — just to give their boots
    a rub
Ere they started operations on the Geebung Polo Club.

Now my readers can imagine how the contest ebbed and flowed,
When the Geebung boys got going it was time to clear the road;
And the game was so terrific that ere half the time was gone
A spectator's leg was broken — just from merely looking on.
For they waddied one another till the plain was strewn
    with dead,

While the score was kept so even that they neither got ahead.
And the Cuff and Collar captain, when he tumbled off to die,
Was the last surviving player — so the game was called a tie.

Then the captain of the Geebungs raised him slowly from
    the ground,
Though his wounds were mostly mortal, yet he fiercely
    gazed around;
There was no one to oppose him — all the rest were in a trance,
So he scrambled on his pony for his last expiring chance,
For he meant to make an effort to get victory to his side;
So he struck at goal — and missed it — then he tumbled off
    and died.

* * *

By the old Campaspe River, where the breezes shake the grass,
There's a row of little gravestones that the stockmen never pass,
For they bear a crude inscription saying, "Stranger, drop a tear,
For the Cuff and Collar players and the Geebung boys lie here."
And on misty moonlit evenings, while the dingoes howl around,
You can see their shadows flitting down that phantom
    polo ground;
You can hear the loud collisions as the flying players meet,
And the rattle of the mallets, and the rush of ponies' feet,
Till the terrified spectator rides like blazes to the pub —
He's been haunted by the spectres of the Geebung Polo Club.

Mulga Bill's Bicycle

A.B. "Banjo" Paterson (1864 - 1941)

'Twas Mulga Bill, from Eaglehawk, that caught the cycling craze;
He turned away the good old horse that served him many days;
He dressed himself in cycling clothes, resplendent to be seen;
He hurried off to town and bought a shining new machine;
And as he wheeled it through the door, with air of lordly pride,
The grinning shop assistant said, "Excuse me, can you ride?"

"See here, young man," said Mulga Bill, "from Walgett to the sea,
From Conroy's Gap to Castlereagh, there's none can ride like me.
I'm good all round at everything as everybody knows,
Although I'm not the one to talk — I *hate* a man that blows.
But riding is my special gift, my chiefest, sole delight;
Just ask a wild duck can it swim, a wildcat can it fight.
There's nothing clothed in hair or hide, or built of flesh or steel,
There's nothing walks or jumps, or runs, on axle, hoof, or wheel,
But what I'll sit, while hide will hold and girths and straps
    are tight:
I'll ride this here two-wheeled concern right straight away
    at sight."

'Twas Mulga Bill, from Eaglehawk, that sought his own abode,
That perched above Dead Man's Creek, beside the
    mountain road.
He turned the cycle down the hill and mounted for the fray,
But 'ere he'd gone a dozen yards it bolted clean away.
It left the track, and through the trees, just like a silver streak,
It whistled down the awful slope towards the Dead Man's Creek.

Bush Yarns

It shaved a stump by half an inch, it dodged a big white-box:
The very wallaroos in fright went scrambling up the rocks,
The wombats hiding in their caves dug deeper underground,
As Mulga Bill, as white as chalk, sat tight to every bound.
It struck a stone and gave a spring that cleared a fallen tree,
It raced beside a precipice as close as close could be;
And then as Mulga Bill let out one last despairing shriek
It made a leap of twenty feet into the Dead Man's Creek.

'Twas Mulga Bill, from Eaglehawk, that slowly swam ashore:
He said, "I've had some narrer shaves and lively rides before;
I've rode a wild bull round a yard to win a five-pound bet,
But this was the most awful ride that I've encountered yet.
I'll give that two-wheeled outlaw best; it's shaken all my nerve
To feel it whistle through the air and plunge and buck
        and swerve.
It's safe at rest in Dead Man's Creek, we'll leave it lying still;
A horse's back is good enough henceforth for Mulga Bill."

A Bush Christening

A.B. "Banjo" Paterson (1864 - 1941)

On the outer Barcoo where the churches are few,
    And men of religion are scanty,
On a road never cross'd 'cept by folk that are lost,
    One Michael Magee had a shanty.

Now this Mike was the dad of a ten-year-old lad,
    Plump, healthy, and stoutly conditioned;
He was strong as the best, but poor Mike had no rest
    For the youngster had never been christened,

And his wife used to cry, "If the darlin' should die
    Saint Peter would not recognise him."
But by luck he survived till a preacher arrived,
    Who agreed straightaway to baptise him.

Now the artful young rogue, while they held their collogue,
    With his ear to the keyhole was listenin',
And he muttered in fright while his features turned white,
    "What the divil and all is this christenin'?"

He was none of your dolts, he had seen them brand colts,
    And it seemed to his small understanding,
If the man in the frock made him one of the flock,
    It must mean something very like branding.

So away with a rush he set off for the bush,
    While the tears in his eyelids they glistened—
"'Tis outrageous," says he, "to brand youngsters like me,
    I'll be dashed if I'll stop to be christened!"

Bush Yarns

Like a young native dog he ran into a log,
    And his father with language uncivil,
Never heeding the "praste" cried aloud in his haste,
    "Come out and be christened, you divil!"

But he lay there as snug as a bug in a rug,
    And his parents in vain might reprove him,
Till his reverence spoke (he was fond of a joke)
    "I've a notion," says he, "that'll move him."

"Poke a stick up the log, give the spalpeen a prog;
    Poke him aisy—don't hurt him or maim him,
'Tis not long that he'll stand, I've the water at hand,
    As he rushes out this end I'll name him.

"Here he comes, and for shame! ye've forgotten the name—
    Is it Patsy or Michael or Dinnis?"
Here the youngster ran out, and the priest gave a shout—
    "Take your chance, anyhow, wid 'Maginnis'!"

As the howling young cub ran away to the scrub
    Where he knew that pursuit would be risky,
The priest, as he fled, flung a flask at his head
    That was labelled "Maginnis's Whisky!"

And Maginnis Magee has been made a J.P.,
    And the one thing he hates more than sin is
To be asked by the folk who have heard of the joke,
    How he came to be christened "Maginnis"!

The Man From Snowy River
A.B. "Banjo" Paterson (1864 - 1941)

There was movement at the station, for the word had
 passed around
That the colt from old Regret had got away,
And had joined the wild bush horses — he was worth a
 thousand pound,
So all the cracks had gathered to the fray.
All the tried and noted riders from the stations near and far
Had mustered at the homestead overnight,
For the bushmen love hard riding where the wild bush horses are,
And the stockhorse snuffs the battle with delight.

There was Harrison, who made his pile when Pardon won
 the cup,
The old man with his hair as white as snow;
But few could ride beside him when his blood was fairly up —
He would go wherever horse and man could go.
And Clancy of the Overflow came down to lend a hand,
No better horseman ever held the reins;
For never horse could throw him while the saddle girths
 would stand,
He learnt to ride while droving on the plains.

And one was there, a stripling on a small and weedy beast,
He was something like a racehorse undersized,
With a touch of Timor pony — three parts thoroughbred at least —
And such as are by mountain horsemen prized.
He was hard and tough and wiry — just the sort that won't say die —
There was courage in his quick impatient tread;
And he bore the badge of gameness in his bright and fiery eye,
And the proud and lofty carriage of his head.

Bush Yarns

But still so slight and weedy, one would doubt his power to stay,
And the old man said, "That horse will never do
For a long and tiring gallop — lad, you'd better stop away,
Those hills are far too rough for such as you."
So he waited sad and wistful — only Clancy stood his friend —
"I think we ought to let him come," he said;
"I warrant he'll be with us when he's wanted at the end,
For both his horse and he are mountain bred.

"He hails from Snowy River, up by Kosciusko's side,
Where the hills are twice as steep and twice as rough,
Where a horse's hoofs strike firelight from the flint stones
    every stride,
The man that holds his own is good enough.
And the Snowy River riders on the mountains make their home,
Where the river runs those giant hills between;
I have seen full many horsemen since I first commenced to roam,
But nowhere yet such horsemen have I seen."

So he went — they found the horses by the big mimosa clump —
They raced away towards the mountain's brow,
And the old man gave his orders, "Boys, go at them from the jump,
No use to try for fancy riding now.
And, Clancy, you must wheel them, try and wheel them to
    the right.
Ride boldly, lad, and never fear the spills,
For never yet was rider that could keep the mob in sight,
If once they gain the shelter of those hills."

So Clancy rode to wheel them — he was racing on the wing
Where the best and boldest riders take their place,
And he raced his stockhorse past them, and he made the
    ranges ring
With the stockwhip, as he met them face to face.
Then they halted for a moment, while he swung the dreaded lash,
But they saw their well-loved mountain full in view,
And they charged beneath the stockwhip with a sharp and
    sudden dash,
And off into the mountain scrub they flew.

The Man From Snowy River

Then fast the horsemen followed, where the gorges deep and black
Resounded to the thunder of their tread,
And the stockwhips woke the echoes, and they fiercely answered back
From cliffs and crags that beetled overhead.
And upward, ever upward, the wild horses held their way,
Where mountain ash and kurrajong grew wide;
And the old man muttered fiercely, "We may bid the mob good day,
No man can hold them down the other side."

When they reached the mountain's summit, even Clancy took a pull,
It well might make the boldest hold their breath,
The wild hop scrub grew thickly, and the hidden ground was full
Of wombat holes, and any slip was death.
But the man from Snowy River let the pony have his head,
And he swung his stockwhip round and gave a cheer,
And he raced him down the mountain like a torrent down its bed,
While the others stood and watched in very fear.

He sent the flint stones flying, but the pony kept his feet,
He cleared the fallen timber in his stride,
And the man from Snowy River never shifted in his seat —
It was grand to see that mountain horseman ride.
Through the stringybarks and saplings, on the rough and broken ground,
Down the hillside at a racing pace he went;
And he never drew the bridle till he landed safe and sound,
At the bottom of that terrible descent.

He was right among the horses as they climbed the further hill,
And the watchers on the mountain standing mute,
Saw him ply the stockwhip fiercely, he was right among
    them still,
As he raced across the clearing in pursuit.
Then they lost him for a moment, where two mountain
    gullies met
In the ranges, but a final glimpse reveals
On a dim and distant hillside the wild horses racing yet,
With the man from Snowy River at their heels.

And he ran them single-handed till their sides were white
    with foam.
He followed like a bloodhound on their track,
Till they halted cowed and beaten, then he turned their heads
    for home,
And alone and unassisted brought them back.
But his hardy mountain pony he could scarcely raise a trot,
He was blood from hip to shoulder from the spur;
But his pluck was still undaunted, and his courage fiery hot,
For never yet was mountain horse a cur.

And down by Kosciusko, where the pine-clad ridges raise
Their torn and rugged battlements on high,
Where the air is clear as crystal, and the white stars fairly blaze
At midnight in the cold and frosty sky,
And where around the Overflow the reed-beds sweep and sway
To the breezes, and the rolling plains are wide,
The Man from Snowy River is a household word today,
And the stockmen tell the story of his ride.

Said Hanrahan

John O'Brien (P. J. Hartigan) (1879 - 1952)

"We'll all be rooned," said Hanrahan,
    In accents most forlorn,
Outside the church, ere Mass began,
    One frosty Sunday morn.

The congregation stood about,
    Coat-collars to the ears,
And talked of stock, and crops, and drought,
    As it had done for years.

"It's looking crook," said Daniel Croke;
    "Bedad, it's cruke, me lad,
For never since the banks went broke
    Has seasons been so bad."

"It's dry, all right," said young O'Neil,
    With which astute remark
He squatted down upon his heel
    And chewed a piece of bark.

And so around the chorus ran
    "It's keepin' dry, no doubt."
"We'll all be rooned," said Hanrahan,
    "Before the year is out."

"The crops are done; ye'll have your work
    To save one bag of grain;
From here way out to Back-o'-Bourke
    They're singin' out for rain.

"They're singin' out for rain," he said,
    "And all the tanks are dry."
The congregation scratched its head,
    And gazed around the sky.

Bush Yarns

"There won't be grass, in any case,
    Enough to feed an ass;
There's not a blade on Casey's place
    As I came down to Mass."

"If rain don't come this month," said Dan,
    And cleared his throat to speak —
"We'll all be rooned," said Hanrahan,
    "If rain don't come this week."

A heavy silence seemed to steal
    On all at this remark;
And each man squatted on his heel,
    And chewed a piece of bark.

"We want an inch of rain, we do,"
    O'Neil observed at last;
But Croke "maintained" we wanted two
    To put the danger past.

"If we don't get three inches, man,
    Or four to break this drought,
We'll all be rooned," said Hanrahan,
    "Before the year is out."

In God's good time down came the rain;
    And all the afternoon
On iron roof and window-pane
    It drummed a homely tune.

And through the night it pattered still,
    And lightsome, gladsome elves
On dripping spout and window-sill
    Kept talking to themselves.

Said Hanrahan

It pelted, pelted all day long,
    A-singing at its work,
Till every heart took up the song
    Way out to Back-o'-Bourke.

And every creek a banker ran,
    And dams filled overtop;
"We'll all be rooned," said Hanrahan,
    "If this rain doesn't stop."

And stop it did, in God's good time;
    And spring came in to fold
A mantle o'er the hills sublime
    Of green and pink and gold.

And days went by on dancing feet,
    With harvest-hopes immense,
And laughing eyes beheld the wheat
    Nid-nodding o'er the fence.

And, oh, the smiles on every face,
    As happy lad and lass
Through grass knee-deep on Casey's place
    Went riding down to Mass.

While round the church in clothes genteel
    Discoursed the men of mark,
And each man squatted on his heel,
    And chewed his piece of bark.

"There'll be bush-fires for sure, me man,
    There will, without a doubt;
We'll all be rooned," said Hanrahan,
    "Before the year is out."

The Golden Past

The Golden Past

Clancy of the Overflow

A.B. "Banjo" Paterson (1864 - 1941)

I had written him a letter which I had, for want of better
    Knowledge, sent to where I met him down the Lachlan,
        years ago,
He was shearing when I knew him, so I sent the letter to him,
    Just "on spec", addressed as follows: "Clancy, of The
        Overflow".

And an answer came directed in a writing unexpected,
    (And I think the same was written in a thumbnail dipped
        in tar)
'Twas his shearing mate who wrote it, and *verbatim* I will quote it:
    "Clancy's gone to Queensland droving, and we don't
        know where he are."

          *   *   *

In my wild erratic fancy visions come to me of Clancy
    Gone a-droving "down the Cooper" where the western
        drovers go;
As the stock are slowly stringing, Clancy rides behind them
    singing,
    For the drover's life has pleasures that the townsfolk
        never know.

And the bush hath friends to meet him, and their kindly voices
    greet him
    In the murmur of the breezes and the river on its bars,
And he sees the vision splendid of the sunlit plains extended,
    And at night the wondrous glory of the everlasting stars.

* * *

I am sitting in my dingy little office, where a stingy
> Ray of sunlight struggles feebly down between the
>> houses tall,
And the foetid air and gritty of the dusty, dirty city
> Through the open window floating, spreads its foulness
>> over all.

And in place of lowing cattle, I can hear the fiendish rattle
> Of the tramways and the buses making hurry down the
>> street,
And the language uninviting of the gutter children fighting,
> Comes fitfully and faintly through the ceaseless tramp of
>> feet.

And the hurrying people daunt me, and their pallid faces
> haunt me
>> As they shoulder one another in their rush and nervous
>>> haste,
With their eager eyes and greedy, and their stunted forms
> and weedy,
>> For townsfolk have no time to grow, they have no time to
>>> waste.

And I somehow fancy that I'd like to change with Clancy,
> Like to take a turn at droving where the seasons come
>> and go,
While he faced the round eternal of the cashbook and
> the journal —
>> But I doubt he'd suit the office, Clancy, of "The Overflow".

The Golden Past

The Old Australian Ways

A.B. "Banjo" Paterson (1864 - 1941)

The London lights are far abeam
    Behind a bank of cloud,
Along the shore the gaslights gleam,
    The gale is piping loud;
And down the Channel, groping blind,
    We drive her through the haze
Towards the land we left behind —
The good old land of 'never mind',
    And old Australian ways.

The narrow ways of English folk
    Are not for such as we;
They bear the long-accustomed yoke
    Of staid conservancy:
But all our roads are new and strange,
    And through our blood there runs
The vagabonding love of change
That drove us westward of the range
    And westward of the suns.

The city folk go to and fro
    Behind a prison's bars,
They never feel the breezes blow
    And never see the stars;
They never hear in blossomed trees
    The music low and sweet
Of wild birds making melodies,
Nor catch the little laughing breeze
    That whispers in the wheat.

The Old Australian Ways

Our fathers came of roving stock
    That could not fixed abide:
And we have followed field and flock
    Since e'er we learnt to ride;
By miner's camp and shearing shed,
    In land of heat and drought,
We followed where our fortunes led,
With fortune always on ahead
    And always further out.

The wind is in the barley-grass,
    The wattles are in bloom;
The breezes greet us as they pass
    With honey-sweet perfume;
The parakeets go screaming by
    With flash of golden wing,
And from the swamp the wild-ducks cry
Their long-drawn note of revelry,
    Rejoicing at the Spring.

So throw the weary pen aside
    And let the papers rest,
For we must saddle up and ride
    Towards the blue hill's breast;
And we must travel far and fast
    Across their rugged maze,
To find the Spring of Youth at last,
And call back from the buried past
    The old Australian ways.

The Golden Past

When Clancy took the drover's track
    In years of long ago,
He drifted to the outer back
    Beyond the Overflow;
By rolling plain and rocky shelf,
    With stockwhip in his hand,
He reached at last, oh lucky elf,
The Town of Come-and-Help-Yourself
    In Rough-and-Ready Land.

And if it be that you would know
    The tracks he used to ride,
Then you must saddle up and go
    Beyond the Queensland side —
Beyond the reach of rule or law,
    To ride the long day through,
In Nature's homestead — filled with awe
You then might see what Clancy saw
    And know what Clancy knew.

The Song of Old Joe Swallow

Henry Lawson (1867 - 1922)

When I was up the country in the rough and early days,
I used to work along ov Jimmy Nowlett's bullick-drays;
Then the reelroad wasn't heered on, an' the bush was wild
    an' strange,
An' we useter draw the timber from the saw-pits in the range —
Load provisions for the stations, an' we'd travel far and slow
Through the plains an' 'cross the ranges in the days of long ago.

> *Then it's yoke up the bullicks and tramp beside 'em slow,*
> *An' saddle up yer horses an' a-ridin' we will go,*
> *To the bullick-drivin', cattle-drovin',*
> *Nigger, digger, roarin', rovin'*
> *Days o' long ago.*

Once me and Jimmy Nowlett loaded timber for the town,
But we hadn't gone a dozen mile before the rain come down,
An' me an' Jimmy Nowlett an' the bullicks an' the dray
Was cut off on some risin' ground while floods around us lay;
An' we soon run short of tucker an' terbacca, which was bad,
An' pertaters dipped in honey was the only tuck we had.

An' half our bullicks perished when the drought was on the land,
An' the burnin' heat that dazzles as it dances on the sand;
When the sun-baked clay an' gravel paves for miles the
    burnin' creeks,
An' at ev'ry step yer travel there a rottin' carcase reeks —
But we pulled ourselves together, for we never used ter know
What a feather bed was good for in those days o' long ago.

The Golden Past

But in spite ov barren ridges an' in spite ov mud an' heat,
An' dust that browned the bushes when it rose from
    bullicks' feet,
An' in spite ov cold and chilblains when the bush was white
    with frost,
An' in spite of muddy water where the burnin' plain
    was crossed,
An' in spite of modern progress, and in spite of all their blow,
'Twas a better land to live in, in the days o' long ago.

When the frosty moon was shinin' o'er the ranges like a lamp,
An' a lot of bullick-drivers was a-campin' on the camp,
When the fire was blazin' cheery an' the pipes was drawin' well,
Then our songs we useter chorus an' our yarns we useter tell;
An' we'd talk ov lands we come from, and ov chaps we
    useter know,
For there always was behind us *other* days o' long ago.

Ah, them early days was ended when the reelroad crossed
    the plain,
But in dreams I often tramp beside the bullick-team again:
Still we pauses at the shanty just to have a drop er cheer,
Still I feels a kind ov pleasure when the campin'-ground is near;
Still I smells the old tarpaulin me an' Jimmy useter throw
O'er the timber-truck for shelter in the days ov long ago.

The Song of Old Joe Swallow

I have been a-driftin' back'ards with the changes ov the land,
An' if I spoke ter bullicks now they wouldn't understand,
But when Mary wakes me sudden in the night I'll often say:
'Come here, Spot, an' stan' up, Bally, blank an' blank an'
    come-eer-way.'
An' she says that, when I'm sleepin', oft my elerquince 'ill flow
In the bullick-drivin' language ov the days o' long ago.

Well, the pub will soon be closin', so I'll give the thing a rest;
But if you should drop on Nowlett in the far an' distant west —
An' if Jimmy uses doubleyou instead of ar an' vee,
An' if he drops his aitches, then you're sure to know it's he.
An' yer won't forgit to arsk him if he still remembers Joe
As knowed him up the country in the days o' long ago.

> *Then it's yoke up the bullicks and tramp beside 'em slow,*
> *An' saddle up yer horses an' a-ridin' we will go,*
> *To the bullick-drivin', cattle-drovin',*
> *Nigger, digger, roarin', rovin'*
> *Days o' long ago.*

The Golden Past

They've Builded...

Furnley Maurice (Frank Wilmot) (1881 - 1942)

They've builded wooden timber tracks,
    And a trolly with screaming brakes
Noses into the secret bush,
    Into the birdless brooding bush,
And the tall old gums it takes.

And down in the sunny valley,
    The snorting saw screams slow;
Oh bush that nursed my people,
Oh bush that cursed my people,
That flayed and made my people,
    I weep to watch you go.

Echoes of Wheels...
Furnley Maurice (Frank Wilmot) (1881 - 1942)

Echoes of wheels and singing lashes
    Wake on the morning air;
Out of the kitchen a youngster dashes,
    Giving the ducks a scare.
Three jiffs from house to gully,
    And over the bridge to the gate;
And then a panting little boy
    Climbs on the rails to wait.

For there is long-whipped cursing Bill
    With four enormous logs,
Behind a team with the white-nosed leader's
    Feet in the sucking bogs.
Oh it was great to see them stuck,
    And grand to see them strain,
Until the magical language of Bill
    Had got them out again!

I foxed them to the shoulder turn,
    I saw him work them around,
And die into the secret bush,
    Leaving only sound.

The Golden Past

And it isn't bullocks I recall,
    Nor waggons my memory sees;
But in the scented bush a track
    Turning among the trees.

Not forests of lean towering gums,
    Nor notes of birds and bees,
Do I remember so well as a track
    Turning among the trees.

Oh track where the brown leaves fall
    In dust to our very knees!
And it isn't the wattle that I recall,
Nor the sound of the bullocky's singing lash,
When the cloven hoofs in the puddles splash;
But the rumble of an unseen load,
Swallowed along the hidden road
    Turning among the trees!

Return

'E' (Mary Fullerton) (1868 - 1946)

The ruthless bush is grown along the track,
The rude and ruthless bush—
So that I come again at last,
Through winding weed and willow push.

How busy has the pungent dog-wood been,
The purple peppermint!
The upstart ferns on loamy floor
Show many a spoor and padded print.

I stumble on a little burrowed home,
And chuckles overhead
Bring back my yesterdays until
Nothing of all the past is dead.

All here again, the beast, the bird, the bush,
Expelled for many a year...
If I return, then why not they?
We are all native here.

Colonial Ballads

Colonial Ballads

Jim Jones at Botany Bay

Anon.

O, listen for a moment lads, and hear me tell my tale —
How, o'er the hill from England's shore I was compelled to sail.

The jury says "He's guilty, sir" and says the judge, says he —
"For life, Jim Jones, I'm sending you across the stormy sea;

And take my tip, before you ship to join the Iron-gang,
Don't be too gay at Botany Bay, or else you'll surely hang —

Or else you'll surely hang," says he — "and after that, Jim Jones,
High up upon th' gallow-tree the crows will pick your bones.

You'll have no chance for mischief then; remember what I say,
They'll flog th' poachin' out of you, out there at Botany Bay!"

The winds blew high upon the th' sea, and th' pirates came along,
But the soldiers on our convict ship were full five
    hundred strong.

They opened fire and somehow drove that pirate ship away.
I'd have rather joined that pirate ship than have come to
    Botany Bay:

For night and day the irons clang, and like poor galley slaves
We toil, and toil, and when we die must fill dishonoured graves.

But bye-and-bye I'll break my chains: into the bush I'll go,
And join the brave bushrangers — Jack Donahoe and Co.:

And some dark night when everything is silent in the town
I'll kill the tyrants, one and all; and shoot th' floggers down:

I'll give th' law a little shock: remember what I say,
They'll regret they sent Jim Jones in chains to Botany Bay!

A Convict's Lament on the Death of Captain Logan

Anon.

I am a native of the land of Erin,
And lately banished from that lovely shore;
I left behind my aged parents
And the girl I did adore.
In transient storms as I set sailing,
Like mariner bold my courage did steer;
Sydney Harbour was my destination —
That cursed place at length drew near.

I then joined banquet in congratulation
On my safe arrival from the briny sea;
But, alas, alas! I was mistaken —
Twelve years transportation to Moreton Bay.
Early one morning I carelessly wandered,
By the Brisbane waters I chanced to stray;
I saw a prisoner sadly bewailing,
Whilst on the sunlit banks he lay.

He said, "I've been a prisoner at Port Macquarie,
At Norfolk Island, and Emu Plains;
At Castle Hill and cursed Toongabbie —
At all those places I've worked in chains,
But of all these places of condemnation,
In each penal station of New South Wales,
Moreton Bay I found no equal,
For excessive tyranny each day prevails.

Colonial Ballads

Early in the morning as the day is dawning,
To trace from heaven the morning dew,
Up we started at a moment's warning
Our daily labour to renew.
Our overseer's superintendents —
These tyrants' orders we must obey,
Or else at the triangles our flesh is mangled —
Such are our wages at Moreton Bay!

For three long years I've been beastly treated;
Heavy irons each day I wore;
My poor back from flogging has been lacerated,
And oft-times painted with crimson gore.
Like the Egyptians and ancient Hebrews,
We were sorely oppressed by Logan's yoke,
Till kind Providence came to our assistance,
And gave this tyrant his fatal stroke.

Yes, he was hurried from that place of bondage
Where he thought he would gain renown;
But a native black, who lay in ambush,
Gave this monster his fatal wound.
Fellow prisoners be exhilarated;
Your former sufferings you will not mind,
For it's when from bondage you are extricated
You'll leave such tyrants far behind!"

Colonial Experience

Anon.

When I first came to Sydney Cove
And up and down the streets did rove,
I thought such sights I ne'er did see
Since first I learnt my ABC.

Chorus:
Oh! it's broiling in the morning,
It's toiling in the morning,
It's broiling in the morning,
It's toiling all day long.

Into the park I took a stroll —
I felt just like a buttered roll,
A pretty name "The Sunny South!"
A better one "The Land of Drouth!"

Next day into the bush I went,
On wild adventure I was bent,
Dame Narure's wonders I'd explore,
All thoughts of danger would ignore.

The mosquitoes and bulldog ants
Assailed me even through my pants.
It nearly took my breath away
To hear the jackass laugh so gay!

Colonial Ballads

This lovely country, I've been told,
Abounds in silver and in gold.
You may pick it up all day,
Just as leaves in autumn lay!

Marines will chance this yarn believe,
But bluejackets you can't deceive.
Such pretty stories will not fit,
Nor can I their truth admit.

Some say there's lots of work to do.
Well, yes, but then, 'twixt me and you,
A man may toil and broil all day —
The big, fat man gets all the pay.

Mayhap such good things there may be,
But you may have them all, for me,
Instead of roaming foreign parts
I wish I'd studied the Fine Arts!

Botany Bay Courtship

Anon.

The Currency Lads may fill their glasses,
And drink to the health of the Currency Lasses;
But the lass I adore, the lass for me,
Is the lass in the Female Factory.

O! Molly's her name, and her name is Molly,
Although she was tried by the name of Polly;
She was tried and was cast for death at Newry,
But the Judge was bribed and so we're the Jury.

She got "death recorded" in Newry town,
For stealing her mistress's watch and gown;
Her little boy Paddy can tell you the tale,
His father was turnkey of Newry jail.

The first time I saw the comely lass
Was at Parramatta, going to Mass;
Says I, "I'll marry you now in an hour,"
Says she, "Well, go and fetch Father Power."

But I got into trouble that very same night!
Being drunk on the street I got into a fight,
A constable seized me — I gave him a box —
And was put in the watch-house and then in the stocks.

O! it's very unaisy as I may remember,
To sit in the stocks in the month of December;
With the north wind so hot, and the hot sun right over,
O! sure, and it's no place at all for a lover!

"It's worse than a treadmill," says I, "Mr Dunn,
To sit here all day in the hate of the sun!"
"Either that or a dollar," says he, "for your folly," –
But if I'd a dollar I'd drink it with Molly.

But now I am out again, early and late
I sigh and cry at the Factory gate,
"O! Mrs R, late Mrs F—n,
O! won't you let Molly out very soon?"

"Is it Molly McGuigan?" says she to me,
"Is it not?" says I, for she knowed it was she.
"Is it her you mean that was put in the stocks
"For beating her mistress, Mrs Cox?"

"O! yes and it is, madam, pray let me in,
"I have brought her a half-pint of Cooper's best gin,
"She likes it as well as she likes her own mother,
"O! now let me in, madam, I am her brother."

So the Currency Lads may fill their glasses,
And drink to the health of the Currency Lasses;
But the lass I adore, the lass for me,
Is a lass in the Female Factory.

The Wild Colonial Boy

Anon.

'Tis of a wild Colonial Boy, Jack Doolan was his name,
Of poor but honest parents he was born in Castlemaine.
He was his father's only hope, his mother's only joy,
And dearly did his parents love the wild Colonial Boy.

Chorus:
Come, all my hearties, we'll roam the mountains high,
Together we will plunder, together we will die.
We'll wander over valleys, and gallop over plains,
And we'll scorn to live in slavery, bound down with iron chains.

He was scarcely sixteen years of age when he left his
      father's home,
And through Australia's sunny clime a bushranger did roam.
He robbed those wealthy squatters, their stock he did destroy,
And a terror to Australia was the wild Colonial Boy.

In sixty-one this daring youth commenced his wild career,
With a heart that knew no danger, no foeman did he fear.
He stuck up the Beechworth mail-coach, and robbed
      Judge MacEvoy,
Who trembled, and gave up his gold to the wild Colonial Boy.

Colonial Ballads

He bade the judge "Good morning", and told him to beware,
That he'd never rob a hearty chap that acted on the square,
And never to rob a mother of her son and only joy,
Or else you might turn outlaw, like the wild Colonial Boy.

One day as he was riding the mountain-side along,
A-listening to the little birds, their pleasant laughing song,
Three mounted troopers rode along — Kelly, Davis and FitzRoy —
They thought that they would capture him, the wild Colonial Boy.

"Surrender now, Jack Doolan, you see there's three to one.
Surrender now, Jack Doolan, you a daring highwayman."
He drew a pistol from his belt, and shook the little toy,
"I'll fight, but not surrender," said the wild Colonial Boy.

He fired at Trooper Kelly and brought him to the ground,
And in return from Davis received a mortal wound.
All shattered through the jaws he lay still firing at FitzRoy,
And that's the way they captured him — the wild Colonial Boy.

The Maranoa Drovers

Anon.

The night is dark and stormy, and the sky is clouded o'er;
    We'll saddle up our horses and away,
And we'll yard the squatters' cattle through the darkness of the night,
    And we'll keep them on the camp till break of day.

Chorus:
For we're going, going, going to Gunnedah so far,
    And we'll soon be into sunny New South Wales;
We'll bid farewell to Queensland, with its swampy coolibah —
    Happy drovers from the sandy Maranoa.

When the fires are burning bright through the darkness of the night,
    And the cattle camping quiet, well, I'm sure
That I wish for two o'clock when I call the other watch —
    This is droving from the sandy Maranoa.

Our beds made on the ground, we are sleeping all so sound
    When we're wakened by the distant thunder's roar,
And the lightning's vivid flash, followed by an awful crash —
    It's tough on drovers from the Maranoa.

We are up at break of day, and we're all soon on the way,
    For we always have to go ten miles or more;
It don't do to loaf about, or the squatter will come out —
    He's strict on drovers from the sandy Maranoa.

Oh we'll soon be on the Moonbi, and we'll cross the Barwon, too:
    Then we'll be out upon the rolling plains once more;
And we'll shout "hurrah for Queensland and its swampy coolibah,
    And the cattle that came off the Maranoa!"

Colonial Ballads

The Diggins-Oh

Anon.

I've come back all skin and bone
From the diggins-oh.
And I wish I'd never gone
To the diggins-oh.
Believe me, 'tis no fun,
I once weighed fifteen stone,
But they brought my down to one
At the diggins-oh!

I thought a good home could be found
At the diggins-oh.
But soon I found I got aground
At the diggins-oh.
The natives came one day,
Burnt my cottage down like hay,
With my wife they ran away
To the diggins-oh.

I built a hut with mud
At the diggins-oh.
That got washed away by flood
At the diggins-oh.
I used to dig, and cry
It wouldn't do to die,
Undertakers charge too high
At the diggins-oh.

The Diggins-Oh

I paid for victuals with a frown,
At the diggins-oh.
Three potatoes half a crown,
At the diggins-oh.
Sprats five shillings a dish
If for Dutch plaice you wish,
Two dollars buys that fish
At the diggins-oh.

A crown a pound for steaks,
At the diggins-oh.
Ditto chops, and no great shakes,
At the diggons-oh.
Five "hog" a small pig's cheek;
If herring red you'll seek,
One will keep you dry a week,
At the diggins-oh.

Table beer two bob a quart,
At the diggins-oh.
Get your eyes gouged out for nought,
At the diggins-oh.
Five shillings a four-pound brick,
Butter a shilling a lick,
They never give no tick
At the diggins-oh.

Colonial Ballads

They tied me to a tree,
At the diggins-oh.
With the nuggets they made free,
At the diggins-oh.
I escaped from bodily hurt,
Though they stole my very shirt,
I had to paint myself with dirt,
At the diggins-oh.

I felt quite a ruined man,
At the diggins-oh.
Thinks I, I'll get home, if I can,
From the diggins-oh.
I was always catching cold,
And I've been both bought and sold
Like many more, for gold,
At the diggins-oh.

But now I'm safe returned
From the diggins-oh.
Never more I mean to roam
To the diggins-oh.
It some peoples' fortune mends.
Much on the man depends —
I'd sooner be here with my friends
Than at the diggins-oh.

New Landscapes

The Kangaroo
Barron Field (1786 - 1846)

Kangaroo, Kangaroo!
Thou Spirit of Australia,
That redeems from utter failure,
From perfect desolation,
And warrants the creation
Of this fifth part of the Earth,
Which would seem an after-birth,
Not conceiv'd in the Beginning
(For GOD bless'd His work at first,
And saw that it was good),
But emerg'd at the first sinning,
When the ground was therefore curst; —
And hence this barren wood!

Kangaroo, Kangaroo!
Tho' at first sight we should say,
In thy nature that there may
Contradiction be involv'd,
Yet, like discord well resolv'd,
It is quickly harmoniz'd.
Sphynx or mermaid realiz'd,
Or centaur unfabulous,
Would scarce be more prodigious,
Or Pegasus poetical,
Or hippogriff — chimeras all!
But, what Nature would compile,
Nature knows to reconcile;
And Wisdom, ever at her side,
Of all her children's justified.

The Kangaroo

She had made the squirrel fragile;
She had made the bounding hart;
But a third so strong and agile
Was beyond ev'n Nature's art;
So she join'd the former two
    In thee, Kangaroo!
To describe thee, it is hard:
Converse of the camèlopard,
Which beginneth camel-wise,
But endeth of the panther size,
Thy fore half, it would appear,
Had belong'd to some "small deer,"
Such as liveth in a tree;
By thy hinder, thou should'st be
A large animal of chace,
Bounding o'er the forest's space; —
Join'd by some divine mistake,
None but Nature's hand can make —
Nature, in her wisdom's play,
On Creation's holiday.

For howsoe'er anomalous,
Thou yet art not incongruous,
Repugnant or preposterous.
Better-proportion'd animal,
More graceful or ethereal,
Was never follow'd by the hound,
With fifty steps to thy one bound.
Thou can'st not be amended: no;
Be as thou art; thou best art so.

When sooty swans are once more rare,
And duck-moles the Museum's care,
Be still the glory of this land,
Happiest Work of finest Hand!

New Landscapes

A Hot Day in Sydney

Anon.

O this weather! this weather!
    It's more than a mortal can bear;
I fear we shall all melt together,
    So dreadfully hot is the air.

On rising from bed in the morning,
    You feel yourself thirsty and hot;
And while at the toilette adorning,
    You're helpless as though you'd been shot.

You get through the work with great trouble —
    The shave, and the wash, and the dress;
And then comes your breakfast, to double
    The causes of former distress.

The coffee, the tea, and the butter,
    The smoking-hot muffin and bread —
Although you have put to the shutter —
    Invite you in vain to be fed.

The tea and the coffee are hissing,
    The butter is melting away, —
The flies in the milk-jug are kissing,
    The ants in the sugar-bowl play: —

You rise in disgust from the table,
    And with your umbrella unfurl'd,
You toddle as well you you're able,
    To the haunts of the mercantile world.

But whether you sit in your office,
    Or stroll to the market and shops,
To bargain for sugars or coffees,
    For snuff, or tobacco, or hops; —

A Hot Day in Sydney

You still are by no means forgetting
    The torments inflicted by heat —
For still you are puffing and sweating,
    And longing for some cool retreat.

You wash in Cologn's cooling water, —
    You swallow some brisk ginger-beer —
You say to some kind neighbour's daughter,
    "O give me some swizzle, my dear!"

You go to the luncheon at BAX's,
    And call for cool jellies and buns —
But hotter and hotter it waxes, —
    The jelly to liquid soon runs; —

His dainties are only a pester,
    And so you withdraw from his shop; —
Loud rages to the fiery North-wester,
    As back to your office you pop.

The streets are with dust so beclouded,
    You cannot see over the way;
The town is so perfectly shrowded,
    You scarcely believe it is day.

At length comes the wish'd hour of dinner;
    Away to your dwelling you go —
But still you are far from a winner,
    The table displeases you so.

The poultry, the beef, and the mutton,
    The cabbage, potatoes, and peas, —
Though cook'd to delight e'en a glutton,
    Your palate in no degree please: —

The porter, the wine, and the brandy,
    Invite you to wet your parch'd lips,
And being so perfectly handy,
    You take a succession of sips: —

But then your blood burns into fever,
    And sets the whole system on fire, —
And finding the drink a deceiver,
    You soon from the table retire.

The drawing-room then you proceed to,
    And join in the ladies' discourse;
But the heat will not let you give heed to
    The topics their sweet lips enforce.

They offer you tea, bread, and butter,
    And other good things on the tray;
But while you your gratitude mutter,
    The tea-things you wish far away.

They press the piano, with fingers
    So graceful, so taper, so fair,
That while on the scene your heart lingers,
    At the heat you are tempted to swear.

And while they are busily fanning,
    Their beautiful faces and necks,
To please them you fain would be planning,
    Did the heat not so cruelly vex.

A Hot Day in Sydney

At length you retire to your pillow,
    And hope for some comfort in sleep; —
But you toss like a tempest-wrought billow,
    And cannot in one posture keep.

The heat almost stops your respiring —
    The blanket and quilt you kick off; —
The peace that you had hoped in retiring,
    You deplore in a yawn and a cough.

Mosquitos keep humming and stinging;
    Alighting all over your face; —
The cricket and locust are singing,
    And sleep flees your eyelids apace.

And there you be tossing and tumbling,
    So beated, and bitten and stung,
So weary of puffing and grumbling, —
    You are ready to wish yourself hung.

And such are the pleasures of summer,
    In this Australasian land; —
How charming to every new-comer,
    If thus they can charm an old hand!

But still I would bear it with patience,
    And so I would recommend you —
Convinc'd that, of all the earth's nations,
    Not one would be *faultless too.*

New Landscapes

The Beautiful Land of Australia

Anon.

All you on emigration bent,
With home and England discontent,
Come, listen to my sad lament,
    All about the bush of Australia.
I once possessed a thousand pounds.
Thinks I — how very grand it sounds
For a man to be farming his own grounds
    In the beautiful land of Australia.

Chorus
Illawarra, Mittagong,
Parramatta, Wollongong.
If you wish to become an ourang-outang,
Then go the bush of Australia.

Upon the voyage the ship was lost,
In wretched plight I reached the coast,
And was very nigh being made a roast,
    By the savages of Australia.
And in the bush I lighted on
A fierce bushranger with his gun,
Who borrowed my garments, every one,
    For himself in the bush of Australia.

Chorus
Illawarra, Mittagong,
Parramatta, Wollongong.
If you wish to become an ourang-outang
Then go to the bush of Australia.

Sydney town I reached at last,
And now, thinks I, all danger's past,
And shall I make my fortune fast
    In this promising land of Australia.
I quickly went with cash in hand,
Upon the map I chose my land.
When I got there 'twas barren sand
    In the beautiful land of Australia.

Chorus
Illawara, Mittagong,
Parramatta, Wollongong.
If you wish to become an ourang-outang
Then go to the bush of Australia.

Of sheep I got a famous lot.
Some died of hunger, some of rot,
For the devil a drop of rain they got,
    In this flourishing land of Australia.
My convict men were always drunk,
They kept me in a constant funk,
Says I to myself, as to bed I slunk,
    How I wish I was out of Australia!

Chorus
Booligal, Gobarralong,
Emu Flat and Jugiong.
If you wish to become an ourang-outang,
Then go to the bush of Australia.

Of ills, enough I've had you'll own.
And then at last, my woes to crown,
One night my log house was blown down
    That settled us all in Australia.
And now of home and all bereft,
The horrid spot I quickly left,
Making it over by deed of gift
    To the savages of Australia.

Chorus
Booligal, Gobarralong,
Emu Flat and Jugiong.
If you wish to become an ourang-outang,
Then go to the bush of Australia.

I gladly worked my passage home,
And now to England back I've come,
Determined never more to roam,
    At least, to the bush of Australia.
And stones upon the road I'll break,
And earn my seven bob a week,
Which is surely better than the freak
    Of settling down in Australia.

Chorus
Currabubula, Bogolong,
Ulladulla, Gerringong.
If you wouldn't become an ourang-outang,
Don't go to the bush of Australia.

Where the Pelican Builds

Mary Hannay Foott (1846 - 1918)

The horses were ready, the rails were down,
    But the riders lingered still —
        One had a parting word to say,
    And one had his pipe to fill.
Then they mounted, one with a granted prayer,
    And one with a grief unguessed.
        "We are going," they said, as they rode away —
    "Where the pelican builds her nest!"

They had told us of pastures wide and green,
    To be sought past the sunset's glow;
        Of rifts in the ranges by opal lit;
    And gold 'neath the river's flow.
And thirst and hunger were banished words
    When they spoke of that unknown West;
        No drought they dreaded, no flood they feared,
    Where the pelican builds her nest!

The creek at the ford was but fetlock deep
    When we watched them crossing there;
        The rains have replenished it thrice since then,
    And thrice has the rock lain bare.
But the waters of Hope have flowed and fled,
    And never from blue hill's breast
        Come back — by the sun and the sands
            devoured —
    Where the pelican builds her nest.

New Landscapes

Song of the Shingle-Splitters
Henry Kendall (1839 - 1882)

In dark wild wood, where the lone owl broods
And the dingoes nightly yell;
Where the curlew's cry goes floating by,
We splitters of shingles dwell.
And all day through, from the time of the dew
To the hour when the mopoke calls,
Our mallets ring where the wood-birds sing
Sweet hymns by the waterfalls.
And all night long we are lulled by the song
Of gales in the grand old trees;
And in the brakes we can hear the lakes
And the moan of the distant seas.
       For afar from heat and dust of street,
       And hall and turret and dome,
       In forest deep, where the torrents leap,
       Is the shingle-splitter's home.

The dweller in town may lie upon down,
And own his palace and park:
We envy him not his prosperous lot,
Though we slumber on sheets of bark.
Our food is rough, but we have enough;
Our drink is better than wine:
For cool creeks flow wherever we go,
Shut in from the hot sunshine.
Though rude our roof, it is weatherproof,
And at the end of the days
We sit and smoke over yarn and joke,
By the bush-fire's sturdy blaze.
       For away from din and sorrow and sin,
       Where troubles but rarely come,
       We jog along, like a merry song,
       In the shingle-splitter's home.

Song of the Shingle-Splitters

What though our work be heavy, we shirk
From nothing beneath the sun;
And toil is sweet to those who can eat
And rest when the day is done.
In the Sabbath-time we hear no chime,
No sound of the Sunday bells;
But yet Heaven smiles on the forest aisles,
And God in the woodland dwells.
We listen to notes from the million throats
Of chorister birds on high,
Our psalm is the breeze in the lordly trees,
And our dome is the broad, blue sky.
        Oh! a brave, frank life, unsmitten by strife,
        We live wherever we roam,
        And our hearts are free as the great, strong sea,
        In the shingle-splitter's home.

Bell-Birds

Henry Kendall (1839 - 1882)

By channels of coolness the echoes are calling,
And down the dim gorges I hear the creek falling:
It lives in the mountain where moss and the sedges
Touch with their beauty the banks and the ledges.
Through breaks of the cedar and sycamore bowers
Struggles the light that is love to the flowers;
And, softer than slumber, and sweeter than singing,
The notes of the bell-birds are running and ringing.

The silver-voiced bell-birds, the darlings of daytime!
They sing in September their songs of the May-time;
When shadows wax strong, and the thunder-bolts hurtle,
They hide with their fear in the leaves of the myrtle;
When rain and the sunbeams shine mingled together,
They start up like fairies that follow fair weather;
And straightway the hues of their feathers unfolden
Are the green and the purple, the blue and the golden.

October, the maiden of bright yellow tresses,
Loiters for love in these cool wildernesses;
Loiters, knee-deep, in the grasses, to listen,
Where dripping rocks gleam and the leafy pools glisten:
Then is the time when the water-moons splendid
Break with their gold, and are scattered or blended
Over the creeks, till the woodlands have warning
Of songs of the bell-bird and wings of the Morning.

Bell-Birds

Welcome as waters unkissed by the summers
Are the voices of bell-birds to thirsty far-comers.
When fiery December sets foot in the forest,
And the need of the wayfarer presses the sorest,
Pent in the ridges for ever and ever
The bell-birds direct him to spring and to river,
With ring and with ripple, like runnels whose torrents
Are toned by the pebbles and the leaves in the currents.

Often I sit, looking back to a childhood,
Mixt with the sights and the sounds of the wildwood,
Longing for power and the sweetness to fashion
Lyrics with beats like the heart-beats of Passion; —
Songs interwoven of lights and of laughters
Borrowed from bell-birds in far forest-rafters;
So I might keep in the city and alleys
The beauty and strength of the deep mountain valleys:
Charming to slumber the pain of my losses
With glimpses of creeks and a vision of mosses.

Dawn And Sunrise in the Snowy Mountains
Charles Harpur (1813 - 1868)

A few thin strips of fleecy cloud lie long
And motionless above the eastern steeps,
Like shreds of silver lace: till suddenly,
Out from the flushing centre to the ends
On either hand, their lustrous layers become
Dipt all in crimson streaked with pink and gold;
And then, at last, are edged as with a band
Of crystal fire. And now, even long before
The Sun himself is seen, off tow'rds the west
A range of mighty summits, more and more,
Blaze, each like a huge cresset, in the keen
Clear atmosphere. As if the Spirit of Light,
Advancing swiftly thence, and eastward still,
Kept kindling then in quick succession; — till
The universal company of cones
And pyramidal peaks, stand burning all
With rosy fires, like a wide ranging circ
Of God-great altars, — and even so announce
The Sun that now, with a vast flash, is seen
Pushing his rim above yon central height.

A Midsummer Noon
in the Australian Forest

Charles Harpur (1813 - 1868)

Not a bird disturbs the air,
There is quiet everywhere;
Over plains and over woods
What a mighty stillness broods.

   Even the grasshoppers keep
Where the coolest shadows sleep;
Even the busy ants are found
Resting in their pebbled mound;
Even the locust clingeth now
In silence to the barky bough:
And over hills and over plains
Quiet, vast and slumbrous, reigns.

   Only there's a drowsy humming
From yon warm lagoon slow coming:
'Tis the dragon-hornet — see!
All bedaubed resplendently
With yellow on a tawny ground —
Each rich spot nor square nor round,
But rudely heart-shaped, as it were
The blurred and hasty impress there,

Of a vermeil-crusted seal
Dusted o'er with golden meal:
Only there's a droning where
Yon bright beetle gleams the air —
Gleams it in its droning flight
With a slanting track of light,
Till rising in the sunshine higher,
Till its shards flame out like gems on fire.

    Every other thing is still,
Save the ever wakeful rill,
Whose cool murmur only throws
A cooler comfort round Repose;
Or some ripple in the sea
Of leafy boughs, where, lazily,
Tired Summer, in her forest bower
Turning with the noontide hour,
Heaves a slumbrous breath, ere she
Once more slumbers peacefully.

0 'tis easeful here to lie
Hidden from Noon's scorching eye,
In this grassy cool recess
Musing thus of Quietness.

The West Coasters (Tasmania)
Marie E. J. Pitt (1869 - 1948)

Australia sings her Over-land,
    From Murray back to Bourke,
Her three-mile tracks, her sun and sand,
    Her men that do the work;
But here's to them, fill high the glass,
    Who breasted drifting snow,
Tramping though the button-grass...
    Forty years ago!

From Emu Bay to Williamsford,
    From Strahan to Dundas,
Through horizontal scrubs they bored,
    And quaking black morass.
Old Bischoff saw their camp-fires pass,
    Mount Lyell saw them grow;
Tramping through the button-grass...
    Forty years ago!

The bleak winds flayed them as they strode,
    The black frosts bit them sore,
But still The Road, The Open Road
    Went singing on before;
And with them went a lightsome lass,
    Adventure, face aglow,
Tramping through the button-grass...
    Forty years ago!

When red their leaping camp-fires roared
    To forest legions thinned,
The Axe flung, like a levin sword,
    Her challenge down the wind.
They slew the pine and sassafras,
    The myrtle host laid low,
Tramping through the button-grass...
    Forty years ago!

From out their dreams the cities rose
    As yet from hill-heads grey
The first red flush of morning grows
    Into the lord of day.
So here's to them! fill high the glass!
    "The West Coast Esquimaux"
Tramping through the button-grass...
    Forty years ago.

A Gallop of Fire

Marie E. J. Pitt (1869 - 1948)

When the north wind moans thro' the blind creek courses
    And revels with harsh hot sand,
I loose the horses, the wild, red horses.
I loose the horses, the mad, red horses,
    And terror is on the land.

With prophetic murmur the hills are humming,
    The forest-kings bend and blow;
With hoofs of brass on the baked earth drumming,
O brave red horses, they hear us coming,
    And the legions of Death lean low.

O'er the wooded height, and the sandy hollow
    Where the boles to the axe have rung,
Tho' they fly the foeman as flies the swallow,
The fierce red horses, my horses, follow
    With flanks to the faint earth flung.

Or with the frenzied hieroglyphs, fear embossing
    Night's sable horizon bars,
Thro' tangled mazes of death-darts crossing,
I swing my leaders and watch them tossing
    Their red manes against the stars.

But when South winds sob in the drowned creek courses
    And whisper to hard wet sand,
I hold the horses, the spent, red horses,
I hold the horses, the tired, red horses,
And silence is on the land.

Yea, the South wind sobs 'mong the drowned creek courses
    For sorrows no man shall bind —
Ah, God! for the horses, the black plumed horses,
Dear God! for the horses, Death's own pale horses,
    That raced in the tracks behind.

On the Derwent

Frank Penn-Smith (1863-1935)

Pale the evening falls,
Desolate are the darkened hills,
Vast the rippling river flows
Silently away.

Slow the night clouds go
Over the motionless under-calm,
Ebbing in a ceaseless tide
Silently away.

Low the wild duck calls,
Swiftly wavering o'er the wet,
Chains of dark birds rise and fall
Silently away.

Desolate all the world,
Desolately the waters flow,
Swaying in a mystic dance,
Silently away.

The Poor, Poor Country

John Shaw Neilson (1872 - 1942)

Oh 'twas a poor country, in Autumn it was bare,
The only green was the cutting grass and the sheep found
    little there.
Oh, the thin wheat and the brown oats were never two foot high,
But down in the poor country no pauper was I.

My wealth it was the glow that lives forever in the young,
'Twas on the brown water, in the green leaves it hung.
The blue cranes fed their young all day—how far in a tall tree!
And the poor, poor country made no pauper of me.

I waded out to the swan's nest—at night I heard them sing,
I stood amazed at the Pelican, and crowned him for a king;
I saw the black duck in the reeds, and the spoonbill on the sky,
And in that poor country no pauper was I.

The mountain-ducks down in the dark made many a
    hollow sound,
I saw in sleep the Bunyip creep from the waters underground.
I found the plovers' island home, and they fought right valiantly,
Poor was the country, but it made no pauper of me.

New Landscapes

My riches all went into dreams that never yet came home,
They touched upon the wild cherries and the slabs of
    honeycomb,
They were not of the desolate brood that men can sell or buy,
Down in that poor country no pauper was I.

                    ✲ ✲ ✲

The New Year came with heat and thirst and the little lakes
    were low,
The blue cranes were my nearest friends and I mourned to see
    them go;
I watched their wings so long until I only saw the sky,
Down in that poor country no pauper was I.

My Country

Dorothea Mackellar (1885 - 1968)

The love of field and coppice,
    Of green and shaded lanes,
Of ordered woods and gardens
    Is running in your veins.
Strong love of grey-blue distance,
    Brown streams and soft, dim skies—
I know but cannot share it,
    My love is otherwise.

I love a sunburnt country,
    A land of sweeping plains,
Of ragged mountain ranges,
    Of droughts and flooding rains.
I love her far horizons,
    I love her jewel-sea,
Her beauty and her terror—
    The wide brown land for me!

The stark white ring-barked forests,
    All tragic to the moon,
The sapphire-misted mountains,
    The hot gold hush of noon.
Green tangle of the brushes,
    Where lithe lianas coil,
And orchids deck the tree-tops
    And ferns the warm dark soil.

Core of my heart, my country!
    Her pitiless blue sky,
When sick at heart, around us,
    We see the cattle die—
But then the grey clouds gather,
    And we can bless again
The drumming of an army,
    The steady, soaking rain.

Core of my heart, my country!
    Land of the Rainbow Gold,
For flood and fire and famine,
    She pays us back three-fold;
Over the thirsty paddocks,
    Watch, after many days,
The filmy veil of greenness
    That thickens as we gaze...

An opal-hearted country,
    A wilful, lavish land—
All you who have not loved her,
    You will not understand—
Though earth holds many splendours,
    Wherever I may die,
I know to what brown country
    My homing thoughts will fly.

The Banksia
Wolfe Fairbridge (1918 - 1950)

The spear blades of the Xamias are erect
And menacing, slanting from the direct
Drive of the wind where it rubs the dried skull
Of the hill; and below that single gull
Harries the ridges of the approaching sea.
The banksia, all knots and tangles, is less tree
Than the crushed roots of an upturned thornbush —
Disorganized and bare; its straggling brush
Of leaves seem a poor instrument to achieve
That growth of wood. Does it too wish to leave
The place where fortune dropped a seed? Unwind
Its fingers from the soil, and further back find
Space between the the giant strides of the jarrah;
And under those august eyes, a stranger
Be, waiting—waiting for a voice before
The window, and the knock upon the door.

Personal Visions

The Banks of the Condamine

Anon.

Oh, hark the dogs are barking, love,
I can no longer stay,
The men are all gone mustering
And it is nearly day.
And I must off by the morning light
Before the sun doth shine,
To meet the Sydney shearers
On the banks of the Condamine.

Oh Willie, dearest Willie,
I'll go along with you.
I'll cut off all my auburn fringe
And be a shearer too,
I'll cook and count your tally, love,
While ringer-o you shine,
And I'll wash your greasy moleskins
On the banks of the Condamine.

Oh, Nancy, dearest Nancy,
With me you cannot go,
The squatters have given orders, love,
No woman should do so;
Your delicate constitution
Is not equal unto mine,
To stand the constant tigering
On the banks of the Condamine.

The Banks of the Condamine

Oh Willie, dearest Willie,
Then stay back home with me,
We'll take up a selection
And a farmer's wife I'll be:
I'll help you husk the corn, love,
And cook your meals so fine
You'll forget the ram-stag mutton
On the banks of the Condamine.

Oh, Nancy, dearest Nancy,
Please do not hold me back,
Down there the boys are waiting,
And I must be on the track;
So there's a good-bye kiss, love,
Back home here I'll incline
When we've shore the last of the jumbucks
On the banks of the Condamine.

Emus

'E' (Mary Fullerton) (1868 - 1946)

My annals have it so:
A thing my mother saw,
Nigh eighty years ago,
With happiness and awe.

Along a level hill —
A clearing in wild space.
And night's last tardy chill
Yet damp on morning's face.

Sight never to forget:
Solemn against the sky
In stately silhouette
Ten emus walking by.

One after one they went
In line, and without haste:
On their unknown intent,
Ten emus grandly paced.

She, used to hedged-in fields
Watched them go filing past
Into the great Bush Wilds
Silent and vast.

Sudden that hour she knew
That this far place was good,
This mighty land and new
For the soul's hardihood.

For hearts that love the strange,
That carry wonder;
The Bush, the hills, the range,
And the dark flats under.

Because She Would Ask Me Why I Loved Her

Christopher John Brennan (1870 - 1932)

If questioning could make us wise
no eyes would ever gaze in eyes;
if all our tale were told in speech
no mouths would wander each to each.

Were spirits free from mortal mesh
and love not bound in hearts of flesh
no aching breasts would yearn to meet
and find their ecstasy complete.

For who is there that loves and knows
the secret powers by which he grows?
Were knowledge all, what were our need
to thrill and faint and sweetly bleed?

Then seek not, sweet, the *If* and *Why*
I love you now until I die:
For I must love because I live
And life in me is what you give.

A Gray and Dusty Daylight Flows

Christopher John Brennan (1870 - 1932)

A gray and dusty daylight flows
athwart the shatter'd traceries,
pale absence of the ruin'd rose.

Here once, on labour-harden'd knees,
beneath the kindly vaulted gloom
that gather'd them in quickening ease,

They saw the rose of heaven bloom,
alone, in heights of musky air,
with many an angel's painted plume.

So, shadowing forth their dim-felt prayer,
the daedal glass compell'd to grace
the outer day's indifferent stare,

Where now its disenhallow'd face
beholds the petal-ribs enclose
nought, in their web of shatter'd lace,

Save this pale absence of the rose.

Fire in the Heavens
Christopher John Brennan (1870 - 1932)

Fire in the heavens, and fire along the hills,
and fire made solid in the flinty stone,
thick-mass'd or scatter'd pebble, fire that fills
the breathless hour that lives in fire alone.

This valley, long ago the patient bed
of floods that carv'd its antient amplitude,
in stillness of the Egyptian crypt outspread,
endures to drown in noon-day's tyrant mood.

Behind the veil of burning silence bound,
vast life's innumerous busy littleness
is hush'd in vague-conjectured blur of sound
that dulls the brain with slumbrous weight, unless

some dazzling puncture let the stridence throng
in the cicada's torture-point of song.

Personal Visions

The Smoker Parrot

John Shaw Neilson (1872 - 1942)

He has the full moon on his breast,
The moonbeams are about his wing;
He has the colours of a king.
I see him floating unto rest
When all eyes wearily go west,
And the warm winds are quieting.
The moonbeams are about his wing;
He has the full moon on his breast.

Song Be Delicate

John Shaw Neilson (1872 - 1942)

Let your song be delicate.
    The skies declare
No war—the eyes of lovers
    Wake everywhere.

Let your voice be delicate.
    How faint a thing
Is Love, little Love crying
    Under the Spring.

Let your song be delicate.
    The flowers can hear:
Too well they know the tremble
    Of the hollow year.

Let your voice be delicate.
    The bees are home:
All their day's love is sunken
    Safe in the comb.

Let your song be delicate.
    Sing no loud hymn:
Death is abroad ... Oh, the black season!
    The deep—the dim!

Native Companions Dancing
John Shaw Neilson (1872 - 1942)

On the blue plains in wintry days
    These stately birds move in the dance.
Keen eyes have they, and quaint old ways
On the blue plains in wintry days.
The Wind, their unseen Piper, plays,
    They strut, salute, retreat, advance;
On the blue plains, in wintry days,
    These stately birds move in the dance.

The Orange Tree

John Shaw Neilson (1872 - 1942)

The young girl stood beside me. I
    Saw not what her young eyes could see:
— A light, she said, not of the sky
    Lives somewhere in the Orange Tree.

— Is it, I said, of east or west?
    The heartbeat of a luminous boy
Who with his faltering flute confessed
    Only the edges of his joy?

Was he, I said, borne to the blue
    In a mad escapade of Spring
Ere he could make a fond adieu
    To his love in the blossoming?

— Listen! the young girl said. There calls
    No voice, no music beats on me;
But it is almost sound: it falls
    This evening on the Orange Tree.

— Does he, I said, so fear the Spring
    Ere the white sap too far can climb?
See in the full gold evening
    All happenings of the olden time?

Personal Visions

    Is he so goaded by the green?
        Does the compulsion of the dew
    Make him unknowable but keen
        Asking with beauty of the blue?

    — Listen! the young girl said. For all
        Your hapless talk you fail to see
    There is a light, a step, a call
        This evening on the Orange Tree.

    — Is it, I said, a waste of love
        Imperishably old in pain,
    Moving as an affrighted dove
        Under the sunlight or the rain?

    Is it a fluttering heart that gave
        Too willingly and was reviled?
    Is it the stammering at a grave,
        The last word of a little child?

    — Silence! the young girl said. Oh, why,
        Why will you talk to weary me?
    Plague me no longer now, for I
        Am listening like the Orange Tree.

Battlers

Christmas Day near Lake Torrens, 1864

Robert Bruce (1835 - 1908)

But here no merry bells you hear,
    You see no faces bright.
For all is barren, dry and sere,
    Unto the aching sight;

For dust in masses murk and foul
    Drifts by upon the blast,
Which from the south, with dreary howl,
    In gusts come sweeping past.

The people's clothes are dirty, and
    So are their faces too:
They are a listless, grimy band
    As one might wish to view.

There's food in plenty, but 'tis not
    Unwary to be ate,
For swarms of flies and gravy hot
    Are mingled in each plate.

The meat — or rather mutton bones —
    Skin-covered, looks as if
The starving sheep had fed on stones,
    It seems so grim and stiff;

Besides, from total want of fat,
    It has been baked in water;
But as we are well used to that,
    Three men can eat a quarter!

As for the pudding, minus suet,
    And rather underdone,
If we eat much we'll surely rue it,
    For colic is no fun.

Christmas Day near Lake Torrens, 1864

A damper mixed midst drifting sand,
    And rather sodden too,
Completes the entertainment grand
    Set for our long-faced crew.

And then on pudding and on meat
    Fast falls the filthy dust,
Until our meal we cannot eat,
    But leave it in disgust.

We have no heart to dance or sing,
    We have no wish to talk;
We care not to do anything,
    To sit, lay down, or walk.

For thick on the table and on chair,
    On book, on box, on bed,
Dust, filthy dust, is everywhere
    On all things darkly spread.

Our beards and hair are with it fill'd
    Our eyes and ears it bungs;
We breathe it 'till thick mud's distill'd,
    And seems to clog our lungs.

We cannot ride away to seek
    Some valley free from dust,
Our horses are too poor and weak,
    So stay at home we must —

Without we took a stroll; and who
    Would walk on such a day,
Unless he was both fey and fou'
    (Excuse my Scotch, I pray).

We try to read, but vacantly
    We look into each book;
E'en Ingoldsby is soon laid by,
    We laugh not at Nell Cook.

Some try a pipe, and listless eye
    The mingling dust and smoke;
We drain the big tin teapot dry,
    But no one tries to joke,

And so wears on the weary day,
    None are inclined for mirth,
But wish themselves far, far away
    From this vile scene of dearth.

And all are glad when Sol's last ray
    Has faded in the west,
And night in garments dim and grey
    Proclaims the hour of rest.

The wind is gone down with the sun;
    The atmosphere is clear;
We take a glass — a stiffish one,
    Our spirits dull to cheer.

Our dusty rugs we shake and spread,
    Then on their surface lay;
And almost wishing we were dead,
    We end our Christmas Day.

Where The Dead Men Lie

Barcroft Boake (1866 - 1892)

Out on the wastes of the Never Never —
    That's where the dead men lie!
There where the heat-waves dance for ever —
    That's where the dead men lie!
That's where the Earth's loved sons are keeping
Endless tryst: not the west wind sweeping
Feverish pinions can wake their sleeping —
    Out where the dead men lie!

Where brown Summer and Death have mated —
    That's where the dead men die!
Loving with fiery lust unsated —
    That's where the dead men lie!
Out where the grinning skulls bleach whitely
Under the saltbush sparkling brightly;
Out where the wild dogs chorus nightly —
    That's where the dead men lie!

Deep in the yellow, flowing river —
    That's where the dead men die!
Under the banks where the shadows quiver —
    That's where the dead men he!
Where the platypus twists and doubles,
Leaving a train of tiny bubbles;
Rid at last of their earthly troubles —
    That's where the dead men lie!

East and backward pale faces turning —
    That's how the dead men lie!
Gaunt arms stretch with a voiceless yearning —
    That's how the dead men lie!
Oft in the fragrant hush of nooning
Hearing again their mother's crooning,
Wrapt for aye in a dreamful swooning —
    That's how the dead men lie!

Battlers

Only the hand of Night can free them —
    That's when the dead men fly!
Only the frightened cattle see them —
    See the dead men go by!
Cloven hoofs beating out one measure,
Bidding the stockmen know no leisure —
That's when the dead men take their pleasure!
    That's when the dead men fly!

Ask, too, the never-sleeping drover:
    He sees the dead pass by;
Hearing them call to their friends — the plover,
    Hearing the dead men cry;
Seeing their faces stealing, stealing,
Hearing their laughter, pealing, pealing,
Watching their grey forms wheeling, wheeling
    Round where the cattle lie!

Strangled by thirst and fierce privation —
    That's how the dead men die!
Out on Moneygrub's farthest station —
    That's how the dead men die!
Hard-faced greybeards, youngsters callow;
Some mounds cared for, some left fallow;
Some deep down, yet others shallow.
    Some having but the sky.

Moneygrub, as he sips his claret,
    Looks with complacent eye
Down at his watch-chain, eighteen carat —
    There, in his club, hard by:
Recks not that every link is stamped with
Names of the men whose limbs are cramped with
Too long lying in grave-mould, cramped with
    Death where the dead men lie.

Jim's Whip

Barcroft Boake (1866 - 1892)

There it hangs upon the wall
    And never gives a sound,
The hand that trimmed its greenhide fall
    Is hidden underground —
There, in that patch of mallee shade,
    Beneath that grassy mound.

I never take it from the wall,
    That whip belonged to him —
The man I singled from them all,
    He was my husband, Jim;
I see him now — so straight and tall,
    So long and lithe of limb.

That whip was with him night and day
    When he was on the track;
I've often heard him laugh, and say
    That when they heard its crack,
After the breaking of the drought,
    The cattle all came back.

And all the time that Jim was here
    A-working on the run
I'd hear that whip ring, sharp and clear
    Just about set of sun
To let me know that he was near
    And that his work was done.

I was away that afternoon,
    Penning the calves, when — bang!
I heard his whip; 'twas rather soon:
    A thousand echoes rang
And died away among the hills,
    As toward the hut I sprang.

Battlers

I made the tea and waited, but,
    Seized by a sudden whim,
I went and sat outside the hut
    And watched the light grow dim —
I waited there till after dark,
    But not a sign of Jim.

The evening air was damp with dew;
    Just as the clock struck ten
His horse came riderless — I knew
    What was the matter then...
Why should the Lord have singled out
    My Jim from other men?

I took the horse and found him where
    He lay beneath the sky
With blood all clotted in his hair;
    I felt too dazed to cry:
I held him to me, as I prayed
    To God that I might die.

But sometimes now, I seem to hear —
    Just when the air grows chill —
A single whip-crack, sharp and clear,
    Re-echo from the hill.
That's Jim! to let me know he's near
    And thinking of me still.

The Shearer's Wife

Louis Esson (1879 - 1943)

Before the glare o' dawn I rise
To milk the sleepy cows, an' shake
The droving dust from tired eyes,
I set the rabbit traps, then bake
The children's bread.
There 's hay to stook, an' beans to hoe,
Ferns to cut in the scrub below.
Women must work, when men must go
Shearing from shed to shed.

I patch an' darn, now evening comes,
An' tired I am with labour sore,
Tired o' the bush, the cows, the gums,
Tired, but must dree for long months more
What no tongue tells.
The moon is lonely in the sky,
The bush is lonely, an' lonely I
Stare down the track no horse draws nigh
An' start...at the cattle bells.

The Women of the West

George Essex Evans (1863 - 1909)

They left the vine-wreathed cottage and the mansion on the hill,
The houses in the busy streets where life is never still,
The pleasures of the city, and the friends they cherished best:
For love they faced the wilderness — the Women of the West.

The roar, and rush, and fever of the city died away,
And the old-time joys and faces — they were gone for many a day;
In their place the lurching coach-wheel, or the creaking
      bullock chains,
O'er the everlasting sameness of the never-ending plains.

In the slab-built, zinc-roofed homestead of some lately-taken run,
In the tent beside the bankment of a railway just begun,
In the huts on new selections, in the camps of man's unrest,
On the frontiers of the Nation, live the Women of the West.

The red sun robs their beauty, and, in weariness and pain,
The slow years steal the nameless grace that never comes again;
And there are hours men cannot soothe, and words men
      cannot say —
The nearest woman's face may be a hundred miles away.

The Women of the West

The wide Bush holds the secrets of their longing and desires,
When the white stars in reverence light their holy altar-fires,
And silence, like the touch of God, sinks deep into the breast —
Perchance He hears and understands the Women of the West.

For them no trumpet sounds the call, no poet plies his arts —
They only hear the beating of their gallant, loving hearts.
But they have sung with silent lives the song all songs above —
The holiness of sacrifice, the dignity of love.

Well have we held our father's creed. No call has passed us by.
We faced and fought the wilderness, we sent our sons to die.
And we have hearts to do and dare, and yet, o'er all the rest,
The hearts that made the Nation were the Women of the West.

Middleton's Rouseabout

Henry Lawson (1867 - 1922)

Tall and freckled and sandy,
    Face of a country lout;
This was the picture of Andy,
    Middleton's Rouseabout.

Type of a coming nation,
    In the land of cattle and sheep,
Worked on Middleton's station,
    "Pound a week and his keep".

On Middleton's wide dominions
    Plied the stockwhip an' shears;
Hadn't any opinions,
    Hadn't any "idears".

Swiftly the years went over,
    Liquor and drought prevailed;
Middleton went as a drover,
    After his station had failed.

Type of a careless nation,
    Men who are soon played out,
Middleton was: and his station
    Was bought by the Rouseabout.

Flourishing beard and sandy,
    Tall and solid and stout;
This is the picture of Andy,
    Middleton's Rouseabout.

Now on his own dominions
    Works with his overseers;
Hasn't any opinions,
    Hasn't any idears.

Past Carin'

Henry Lawson (1867 - 1922)

Now up and down the sidling brown
    The great black crows are flyin',
And down below the spur, I know,
    Another milker's' dyin';
The crops have withered from the ground,
    The tank's clay bed is glarin',
But from my heart no tear nor sound,
    For I have gone past carin' —
        Past worryin' or carin',
        Past feelin' aught or carin';
        But from my heart no tear nor sound,
        For I have gone past carin'.

Through Death and Trouble, turn about,
    Through hopeless desolation,
Through flood and fever, fire and drought,
    And slavery and starvation;
Through childbirth, sickness, hurt, and blight,
    And nervousness an' scarin',
Through bein' left alone at night,
    I've got to be past carin'.
        Past botherin' or carin',
        Past feelin' and past carin';
        Through city cheats and neighbours' spite,
        I've come to be past carin'.

Battlers

Our first child took, in days like these,
    A cruel week in dyin',
All day upon her father's knees,
    Or on my poor breast lyin';
The tears we shed — the prayers we said
    Were awful, wild — despairin'!
I've pulled three through, and buried two
    Since then — and I'm past carin'.
        I've grown to be past carin',
        Past worryin' and wearin'
        I've pulled three through and buried two
        Since then, and I'm past carin'.

'Twas ten years first, then came the worst,
    All for a barren clearin'
I thought, I thought my heart would burst
    When first my man went shearin';
He's drovin' in the great North-west,
    I don't know how he's farin';
For I, the one that loved him best,
    Have grown to be past carin'.
        I've grown to be past carin'
        Past waitin' and past wearin';
        The girl that waited long ago,
        Has lived to be past carin'.

My eyes are dry, I cannot cry,
    I've got no heart for breakin',
But where it was in days gone by,
    A dull and empty achin'.
My last boy ran away from me —
    I know my temper's wearin' —
But now I only wish to be
    Beyond all signs of carin'.
        Past wearyin' or carin',
        Past feelin' and despairin';
        And now I only wish to be
        Beyond all signs of carin'.

Since the Country Carried Sheep

Harry "Breaker" Morant (1864 - 1902)

We trucked the cows to Homebush, saw the girls, and
    started back,
Went West through Cunnamulla, and got to the Eulo track.
Camped a while at Gonybibil — but, Lord! you wouldn't know
It for the place where you and Mick were stockmen long ago.

Young Merino bought the station, fenced the run and built
    a "shed",
Sacked the stockmen, sold the cattle, and put on sheep instead,
But he wasn't built for Queensland; and every blessed year
One hears of "labour troubles" when Merino starts to shear.

There are ructions with the rouseabouts, and shearers'
    strikes galore!
The likes were never thought of in the cattle days of yore.
And slowly, round small paddocks now, the "sleeping lizards"
    creep,
And Gonybibil's beggared since the country carried sheep.

Time was we had the horses up ere starlight waned away,
The billy would be boiling by the breaking of the day;
And our horses — by Protection — were aye in decent nick,
When we rode up the 'Bidgee where the clearskins
    mustered thick.
They've built *brush-yards* on Wild Horse Creek, where in the
    morning's hush
We've sat silent in the saddle, and listened for the rush
Of the scrubbers — when we heard 'em, 'twas wheel 'em if
    you can,
While gidgee, pine and mulga tried the nerve of horse and man.

Battlers

The mickies that we've branded there! the colts we had to ride!
In Gonybibil's palmy days — before the old boss died.
Could Yorkie Hawkins see his run, I guess his ghost would weep,
For Gonybibil's beggared since the country carried sheep.

From sunrise until sunset through the summer days we'd ride,
But stockyard rails were up and pegged, with cattle safe inside,
When 'twixt the gloamin' and the murk, we heard the
    well-known note —
The peal of boisterous laughter from the kookaburra's throat.

Camped out beneath the starlit skies, the tree-tops overhead,
A saddle for a pillow, and a blanket for a bed,
'Twas pleasant, mate, to listen to the soughing of the breeze,
And learn the lilting lullabies which stirred the mulga-trees.

Our sleep was sound in those times, for the mustering days
    were hard,
The morrows might be harder, with the branding in the yard.
But did you see the station now! the men — and mokes —
    they keep!
You'd own the place was beggared — since the country
    carried sheep.

Butchered to Make a Dutchman's Holiday
Harry "Breaker" Morant (1864 - 1902)

In prison cell I sadly sit
    A d——d crestfallen chappy.
And own to you I feel a bit —
    A little bit — unhappy.

It really ain't the place nor time
    To reel off rhyming diction;
But yet we'll write a final rhyme
    While waiting crucifixion.

No matter what "end" they decide —
    Quick lime? or "b'iling ile?" sir —
We'll do our best when crucified
    To finish off in style, sir!

But we bequeath a parting tip
    For sound advice of such men
As come across in transport ship
    To polish off the Dutchmen.

Battlers

If you encounter any Boers
    You really must not loot 'em,
And, if you wish to leave these shores
    For pity's sake, *don't shoot 'em*.

And if you'd earn a D.S.O. —
    Why every British sinner
Should know the proper way to go
    Is: *Ask the Boer to dinner*.

Let's toss a bumper down our throat
    Before we pass to heaven,
And toast: "The trim-set petticoat
    We leave behind in Devon."

Morant's last poem, written while awaiting execution following his court martial.

The Trenches

Frederic Manning (1882 - 1935)

Endless lanes sunken in the clay,
Bays, and traverses, fringed with wasted herbage,
Seed-pods of blue scabious, and some lingering blooms;
And the sky, seen as from a well,
Brilliant with frosty stars.
We stumble, cursing, on the slippery duck-boards,
Goaded like the damned by some invisible wrath,
A will stronger than weariness, stronger than animal fear,
Implacable and monotonous.

Here a shaft, slanting, and below
A dusty and flickering light from one feeble candle
And prone figures sleeping uneasily,
Murmuring,
And men who cannot sleep.
With faces impassive as masks,
Bright, feverish eyes, and drawn lips,
Sad, pitiless, terrible faces,
Each an incarnate curse.

Here in a bay, a helmeted sentry
Silent and motionless, watching while two sleep,
And he sees before him
With indifferent eyes the blasted and torn land
Peopled with stiff prone forms, stupidly rigid,
And tho' they had not been men.

Dead are the lips where love laughed or sang,
The hands of youth eager to lay hold of life,
Eyes that have laughed to eyes,
And these were begotten,
O love, and lived lightly, and burnt
With the lust of a man's first strength: ere they were rent,
Almost at unawares, savagely; and strewn
In bloody fragments, to be the carrion
Of rats and crows.

And the sentry moves not, searching
Night for menace with weary eyes.

11.11.1918

J. A. R. McKellar (1904 - 1932)

They're bones in full battalions now,
The army underground,
And why should we cry out upon
The dwelling they have found?
Good company it is that they are keeping:
Rich earth below, and grass above them, creeping,
The soldiers, sleeping.

They fought and luck was with them,
When a life was worth the giving.
Day follows day, till one shall find
Them younger than all the living.
Good company it is they are keeping:
I do not think that they would have you weeping,
The soldiers, sleeping.

City Life

The Man from Ironbark
A.B. "Banjo" Paterson (1864 - 1941)

It was the man from Ironbark who struck the Sydney town,
He wandered over street and park, he wandered up and down.
He loitered here, he loitered there, till he was like to drop,
Until at last in sheer despair he sought a barber's shop.
"'Ere! shave my beard and whiskers off, I'll be a man of mark,
I'll go and do the Sydney toff up home in Ironbark."

The barber man was small and flash, as barbers mostly are,
He wore a strike-your-fancy sash, he smoked a huge cigar;
He was a humorist of note and keen at repartee,
He laid the odds and kept a "tote", whatever that may be,
And when he saw our friend arrive, he whispered, "Here's a lark!
Just watch me catch him all alive, this man from Ironbark."

There were some gilded youths that sat along the barber's wall.
Their eyes were dull, their heads were flat, they had no brains
    at all;
To them the barber passed the wink, his dexter eyelid shut,
"I'll make this bloomin' yokel think his bloomin' throat is cut."
And as he soaped and rubbed it in he made a rude remark:
"I s'pose the flats is pretty green up there in Ironbark."

A grunt was all reply he got; he shaved the bushman's chin,
Then made the water boiling hot and dipped the razor in.
He raised his hand, his brow grew black, he paused awhile
    to gloat,
Then slashed the red-hot razorback across his victim's throat:
Upon the newly-shaven skin it made a livid mark —
No doubt it fairly took him in — the man from Ironbark.

The Man From Ironbark

He fetched a wild up-country yell might wake the dead to hear,
And though his throat, he knew full well, was cut from ear
    to ear,
He struggled gamely to his feet, and faced the murd'rous foe
"You've done for me! you dog, I'm beat! one hit before I go!
I only wish I had a knife, you blessed murdering shark!
But you'll remember all your life the man from Ironbark."

He lifted up his hairy paw, with one tremendous clout
He landed on the barber's jaw, and knocked the barber out.
He set to work with nail and tooth, he made the place a wreck;
He grabbed the nearest gilded youth, and tried to break his neck.
And all the while his throat he held to save his vital spark,
And "Murder! Bloody murder!" yelled the man from Ironbark.

A peeler man who heard the din came in to see the show;
He tried to run the bushman in, but he refused to go.
And when at last the barber spoke, and said "'Twas all in
    fun—
'Twas just a little harmless joke, a trifle overdone."
"A joke!" he cried, "By George, that's fine; a lively sort of lark;
I'd like to catch that murdering swine some night in Ironbark."

And now while round the shearing floor the list'ning
    shearers gape,
He tells the story o'er and o'er, and brags of his escape.
"Them barber chaps what keeps a tote, by George,
    I've had enough,
One tried to cut my bloomin' throat, but thank the Lord
    it's tough."
And whether he's believed or no, there's one thing to remark,
That flowing beards are all the go way up in Ironbark.

The Call of Stoush

C.J. Dennis (1876 - 1938)

Wot price ole Ginger Mick? 'E's done a break —
    Gone to the flamin' war to stoush the foe.
Wus it fer glory, or a woman's sake?
    Ar, arst me somethin' easy! I dunno.
'Is Kharki clobber set 'im off a treat,
That's all I know; 'is motive's got me beat.

Ole Mick 'e's trainin' up in Cairo now;
    An' all the cops in Spadger's Lane is sad.
They miss 'is music in the midnight row
    Wot time the pushes mix it good an' glad.
Fer 'e wus one o' them, you understand,
Wot "soils the soshul life uv this fair land."

A peb wus Mick; a leery bloke wus 'e,
    Low down, an' given to the brinnin' cup;
The sort o' chap that coves like you an' me
    Don't mix wiv, 'cos of our strick bringin's-up.
An' 'e wus sich becos unseein' Fate
Lobbed 'im in life a 'undred years too late.

'E wus a man uv vierlence, wus Mick,
    Coarse wiv 'is speech an' in 'is manner low,
Slick wiv 'is 'ands, an' 'andy wiv a brick
    When bricks wus needful to defeat a foe.
An' now 'e's gone an' mizzled to the war,
An' some blokes 'as the nerve to arst "Wot for?"

The Call of Stoush

Wot for? awstruth! 'E wus no patriot
    That sits an' brays advice in days uv strife;
'E never flapped no flags nor sich like rot;
    'E never sung "Gawsave" in all 'is life.
'E wus dispised be them that make sich noise:
But now — O strike! — 'e's "one uv our brave
    boys."

'E's one uv our brave boys, all right, all right.
    'Is early trainin' down in Spadgers Lane
Done 'im no 'arm fer this 'ere orl-in fight:
    'Is loss o' culcher is 'is country's gain.
'Im wiv 'is carst-ir'n chiv an' leery ways —
An' swell tarts 'eavin' 'im sweet words o' praise.

Why did 'e go? 'E 'ad a decent job,
    'Is tart an' 'im they could 'a' made it right.
Why does a wild bull fight to guard the mob?
    Why does a bloomin' bull-ant look fer fight?
Why does a rooster scrap an' flap an' crow?
'E went becos 'e dam well *'ad* to go.

'E never spouted no 'igh-soundin' stuff
    About stern jooty an' 'is country's call;
But, in 'is way, 'e 'eard it right enough
    A-callin' like the shout uv "On the Ball!"
Wot time the footer brings the clicks great joy,
An' Saints or Carlton roughs it up wiv 'Roy.

City Life

The call wot came to cave-men in the days
    When rocks wus stylish in the scrappin' line;
The call wot knights 'eard in the minstrel's lays,
    That sent 'em in tin soots to Palerstine;
The call wot draws all fighters to the fray
It come to Mick, an' Mick 'e must obey...

The Call uv Stoush! ... It's older than the 'ills.
    Lovin' an' fightin' — there's no more to tell
Concernin' men. An' when that feelin' thrills
    The blood uv them 'oo's fathers mixed it well,
They 'ave to 'eed it - bein' 'ow they're built —
As traders 'ave to 'eed the clink uv gilt.

An' them whose gilt 'as stuffed 'em stiff wiv pride
    An' 'aughty scorn uv blokes like Ginger Mick —
I sez to them, put sich crook thorts aside,
    An' don't lay on the patronage too thick.
Orl men is brothers when it comes to lash
An' 'aughty scorn an' Culcher does their lash.

War ain't no giddy garden feete — it's war:
    A game that calls up love an' 'atred both.
An' them that shudders at the sight o' gore,
    An' shrinks to 'ear a drunken soljer's oath,
Must 'ide be'ind the man wot 'eaves the bricks,
An' thank their Gawd for all their Ginger Micks.

The Call of Stoush

Becos 'e never 'ad the chance to find
    The glory o' the world by land an' sea,
Becos the beauty 'idin' in 'is mind
    Wus not writ plain fer blokes like you an' me,
They calls 'im crook; but in 'im I 'ave found
Wot makes a man a man the world around.

Be'ind that dile uv 'is, as 'ard as sin,
    Wus strange, soft thorts that never yet showed out;
An' down in Spadger's Lane, in dirt an' din,
    'E dreamed sich dreams as poits sing about.
'E's 'ad 'is visions uv the Bonzer Tart;
An' stoushed some coot to ease 'is swellin' 'eart.

Lovin' an' fightin' . . . when the tale is told,
    That's all there is to it; an' in their way
Them brave an' noble 'ero blokes uv old
    Wus Ginger Micks — the crook 'uns uv their day.
Jist let the Call uv Stoush give 'im 'is chance
An' Ginger Mick's the 'ero of Romance.

So Ginger Mick 'e's mizzled to the war;
    Joy in 'is 'eart, an' wild dreams in 'is brain;
Gawd 'elp the foe that 'e goes gunnin' for
    If tales is true they tell in Spadger's Lane —
Tales that ud fairly freeze the gentle 'earts
Uv them 'oo knits 'is socks — the Culchered Tarts.

City Life

Washing Day

C.J. Dennis (1876 - 1938)

The little gipsy vi'lits, they wus peepin' thro' the green
As she come walkin' in the grass, me little wife, Doreen.
      The sun shone on the sassafras, where thrushes sung a bar;
      The 'ope an' worry uv our lives wus yelling fer 'is Mar. —
I watched 'er comin' down the green; the sun wus on 'er 'air —
Jist the woman that I marri'd, when me luck wus 'eadin' fair.

I seen 'er walkin' in the sun that lit our little farm;
She 'ad three clothes-pegs in 'er mouth, an' washin' on 'er arm —
      Three clothes-pegs, fer I counted 'em, an' watched 'er as
          she come;
      "The stove-wood's low," she mumbles, "an' young Bill 'as
          cut 'is thumb"
Now, it weren't no giddy love-speech, but it seemed to
    take me straight
Back to the time I kissed 'er first beside 'er mother's gate.

Six years uv wedded life we've 'ad, an' still me dreams is sweet. . .
Aw, them bonzer little vi'lits, they wus smilin' round me feet.
      An' wots a bit uv stove-wood count, wiv paddocks grinnin'
          green,
      When a bloke gits on to dreamin' uv the old days an' Doreen —
The days I thort I snared a saint; but since I've understood
I 'ave wed a dinkum woman, which is fifty times as good.

I 'ave wed a dinkum woman, an' she's give me eyes to see—
Oh, I ain't been mollycoddled, an' there ain't no fluff on me!
    But days when I wus down an' out she seemd so 'igh above;
    An' a saint is made fer worship, but a woman's made fer love.
An' a bloke is growin' richer as sich things 'e comes to know...
(She pegs another sheet an' sez, "The stove-wood's gettin' low.")

A bloke 'e learns a lot uv things in six years wiv a tart;
But thrushes in the sassafras ain't singin' like me 'eart.
    'Tis the thrushes 'oo 'ave tort me in their choonful sort o' way
    That it's best to take things singin' as yeh meet 'em
        day be day;
Fer I wed a reel, live woman, wiv a woman's 'appy knack
Uv torkin' reason inside out an' logic front to back.

An' I like it. 'Struth I like it! Fer a wax doll in a 'ome,
She'd give a man the flamin' pip an' longin's fer to roam.
    Aw, I ain't no silk-sock sookie 'oo ab'ors the rood an' rough;
    Fer, city-born an' gutter-bred, me schoolin' it wus tough.
An' I like the dinkum woman 'oo . . . (She jerks the clothes-prop, so,
An' sez, so sweet an' dangerous, "The stove-wood's gittin' low.")

See, I've studied men in cities, an' I've studied 'em out 'ere;
I've seen 'em 'ard thro' piety an' seen 'em kind thro' beer.
    I've seen the meanest doin' deeds to make the angels smile,
    An' watched the proudest playin' games that crooks 'ud
        reckon vile.
I 'ave studied 'em in bunches an' I've read 'em one be one,
An' there isn't much between 'em when the 'ole thing's
        said an' done.

City Life

An' I've sort o' studied wimmin — fer I've met a tidy few —
An' there's times, when I wus younger, when I kids meself I knew.
> But 'im 'oo 'opes to count the stars or measure up the sea,
> 'E kin 'ave a shot at woman, fer she's fairly flummoxed me...
("I'll 'ave to 'ave *some* wood," she sez, and sez it most perlite
An' secret to a pair uv socks; an' jams a peg in, tight.)

Now, a woman, she's a woman. I 'ave fixed that fer a cert.
They're jist as like as rows uv peas from 'at to 'em uv skirt.
> An' then, they're all so different, yeh find, before yeh've done.
> The more yeh know uv all of 'em the less yeh know uv one.
An' then, the more yeh know uv one...(She gives 'er 'air a touch:
"The stove-wood's nearly done," she sez. "Not that it matters
> *much!*")

The little gipsy vi'lits, they wus smilin' round me feet.
An' this dreamin' dilly day-dreams on a Summer day wus sweet.
> I 'eaves me frame frum orf the fence, an' grabs me little axe;
> But, when I'm 'arf way to the shed, she stops me in me tracks.
"Yer lunch is ready. That ole wood kin easy wait a while."
Strike! I'm marri'd to a woman... But she never seen me smile.

The Play

C.J. Dennis (1876 - 1938)

"Wot's in a name?"— she sez ...An' then she sighs,
An' clasps 'er little 'ands, an' rolls 'er eyes.
"A rose," she sez, "be any other name
Would smell the same.
Oh, w'erefore art you Romeo, young sir?
Chuck yer ole pot, an' change yer moniker!"

Doreen an' me, we bin to see a show—
The swell two-dollar touch. Bong tong, yeh know.
A chair apiece wiv velvit on the seat;
A slap-up treat.
The drarmer's writ be Shakespeare, years ago,
About a barmy goat called Romeo.

"Lady, be yonder moon I swear!" sez 'e.
An' then 'e climbs up on the balkiney;
An' there they smooge a treat, wiv pretty words
Like two love-birds.
I nudge Doreen. She whispers, "Ain't it grand!"
'Er eyes is shining an' I squeeze 'er 'and.

"Wot's in a name?" she sez. 'Struth, I dunno.
Billo is just as good as Romeo.
She may be Juli-er or Juli-et—
'E loves 'er yet.
If she's the tart 'e wants, then she's 'is queen,
Names never count ... But ar, I like "Doreen!"

A sweeter, dearer sound I never 'eard;
Ther's music 'angs around that little word,
Doreen! ... But wot was this I starts to say
About the play?
I'm off me beat. But when a bloke's in love
'Is thorts turns 'er way, like a 'omin' dove.

City Life

This Romeo 'e's lurkin' wiv a crew—
A dead tough crowd o' crooks—called Montague.
'Is cliner's push—wot's nicknamed Capulet—
They 'as 'em set.
Fair narks they are, jist like them back-street clicks,
Ixcep' they fights wiv skewers 'stid o' bricks.

Wot's in a name? Wot's in a string o' words?
They scraps in ole Verona wiv the'r swords,
An' never give a bloke a stray dog's chance,
An' that's Romance.
But when they deals it out wiv bricks an' boots
In Little Lon., they're low, degraded broots.

Wot's jist plain stoush wiv us, right 'ere to-day,
Is "valler" if yer fur enough away.
Some time, some writer bloke will do the trick
Wiv Ginger Mick,
'E'll be a Romeo,
Of Spadger's Lane.
When 'e's bin dead five 'undred years or so.

Fair Juli-et, she gives 'er boy the tip.
Sez she: "Don't sling that crowd o' mine no lip;
An' if you run agin a Capulet,
Jist do a get."
'E swears 'e's done wiv lash; 'e'll chuck it clean.
(Same as I done when I first met Doreen.)

They smooge some more at that. Ar, strike me blue!
It gimme Joes to sit an' watch them two!
'E'd break away an' start to say good-bye,
An' then she'd sigh
"Ow, Ro-me-o!" an' git a strangle-holt,
An' 'ang around 'im like she feared 'e'd bolt.

Nex' day 'e words a gorspil cove about
A secret weddin'; an' they plan it out.
'E spouts a piece about 'ow 'e's bewitched:
Then they git 'itched ...
Now, 'ere's the place where I fair git the pip!
She's 'is for keeps, an' yet 'e lets 'er slip!

Ar! but 'e makes me sick! A fair gazob!
'E's jist the glarsey on the soulful sob,
'E'll sigh and spruik, an' 'howl a love-sick vow—
(The silly cow!)
But when 'e's got 'er, spliced an' on the straight,
'E crools the pitch, an' tries to kid it's Fate.

Aw! Fate me foot! Instid of slopin' soon
As 'e was wed, off on 'is 'oneymoon,
'Im an' 'is cobber, called Mick Curio,
They 'ave to go
An' mix it wiv that push o' Capulets.
They look fer trouble; an' it's wot they gets.

A tug named Tyball (cousin to the skirt)
Sprags 'em an' makes a start to sling off dirt.
Nex' minnit there's a reel ole ding-dong go—
'Arf round or so.
Mick Curio, 'e gets it in the neck,
"Ar rats!" 'e sez, an' passes in 'is check.

Quite natchril, Romeo gits wet as 'ell.
"It's me or you!" 'e 'owls, an' wiv a yell,
Plunks Tyball through the gizzard wiv 'is sword,
'Ow I ongcored!
"Put in the boot!" I sez. "Put in the boot!"
"'Ush!" sez Doreen ... "Shame!" sez some silly coot.

City Life

Then Romeo, 'e dunno wot to do.
The cops gits busy, like they allwiz do,
An' nose around until 'e gits blue funk
An' does a bunk.
They wants 'is tart to wed some other guy.
"Ah, strike!" she sez. "I wish that I could die!"

Now, this 'ere gorspil bloke's a fair shrewd 'ead.
Sez 'e "I'll dope yeh, so they'll *think* yer dead."
(I tips 'e was a cunnin' sort, wot knoo
A thing or two.)
She takes 'is knock-out drops, up in 'er room:
They think she's snuffed, an' plant 'er in 'er tomb.

Then things gits mixed a treat an' starts to whirl.
'Ere's Romeo comes back an' finds 'is girl
Tucked in 'er little coffing, cold an' stiff,
An' in a jiff,
'E swallows lysol, throws a fancy fit,
'Ead over turkey, an' 'is soul 'as flit.

Then Juli-et wakes up an' sees 'im there,
Turns on the water-works an' tears 'er 'air,
"Dear love," she sez, "I cannot live alone!"
An' wiv a moan,
She grabs 'is pockit knife, an' ends 'er cares ...
"*Peanuts or lollies!*" sez a boy upstairs.

The Woman at the Washtub

Victor Daley (1858 – 1905)

The Woman at the Washtub,
    She works till fall of night;
With soap, and suds and soda
    Her hands are wrinkled white.
Her diamonds are the sparkles
    The copper-fire supplies;
Her opals are the bubbles
    That from the suds arise.

The Woman at the Washtub
    Has lost the charm of youth;
Her hair is rough and homely,
    Her figure is uncouth;
Her temper is like thunder,
    With no one she agrees —
The children of the alley
    They cling around her knees.

The Woman at the Washtub
    She too had her romance;
There was a time when lightly
    Her feet flew in the dance.
Her feet were silver swallows,
    Her lips were flowers of fire;
Then she was Bright and Early,
    The Blossom of Desire.

O Woman at the Washtub,
    And do you ever dream
Of all your days gone by in
    Your aureole of steam?
From birth till we are dying
    You wash our sordid duds,
O Woman of the Washtub!
    O Sister of the Suds!

One night I saw a vision
    That filled my soul with dread,
I saw a Woman washing
    The grave-clothes of the dead;
The dead were all the living,
    The dry were lakes and meres,
The Woman at the Washtub
    She washed them with her tears.

I saw a line with banners
    Hung forth in proud array —
The banners of all battles
    From Cain to Judgement Day.
And they were stiff with slaughter
    And blood from hem to hem,
And they were red with glory,
    And she was washing them.

"Who comes forth to the Judgement,
    And who will doubt my plan?"
"I come forth to the Judgement
    And for the Race of Man.
I rocked him in his cradle,
    I washed him for his tomb,
I claim his soul and body,
    And I will share his doom."

The Yellow Gas

Christopher John Brennan (1870 - 1932)

The yellow gas is fired from street to street
past rows of heartless homes and hearths unlit,
dead churches, and the unending pavement beat
by crowds — say rather, haggard shades that flit

round nightly haunts of their delusive dream,
where'er our paradisal instinct starves: —
till on the utmost post, its sinuous gleam
crawls in the oily water of the wharves;

where Homer's sea loses his keen breath, hemm'd
what place rebellious piles were driven down —
the priestlike waters to this task condemn'd
to wash the roots of the inhuman town! —

where fat and strange-eyed fish that never saw
the outer deep, broad halls of sapphire light,
glut in the city's draught each nameless maw:
— and there, wide-eyed unto the soulless night,

methinks a drown'd maid's face might fitly show
what we have slain, a life that had been free,
clean, large, nor thus tormented — even so
as are the skies, the salt winds and the sea.

City Life

Ay, we had saved our days and kept them whole,
to whom no part in our old joy remains,
had felt those bright winds sweeping thro' our soul
and all the keen sea tumbling in our veins,

had thrill'd to harps of sunrise, when the height
whitens, and dawn dissolves in virgin tears,
or caught, across the hush'd ambrosial night,
the choral music of the swinging spheres,

or drunk the silence if nought else — But no!
and from each rotting soul distil in dreams
a poison, o'er the old earth creeping slow,
that kills the flowers and curdles the live streams,

that taints the fresh breath of re-risen day
and reeks across the pale bewildered moon:
— shall we be cleans'd and how? I only pray,
red flame or deluge, may that end be soon!

Football Field: Evening

J. A. R. McKellar (1904 - 1932)

Cross bars and posts, the echo of distant bells,
The cool and friendly scent of whispering turf;
And in the air a little wind that tells
Of moonlit waves beyond a murmuring surf.

The glittering blue and verdant afternoon
Has locked up all its colours, leaving dearth,
Deserted, underneath a careless moon,
The glory has departed from this earth.

The goals stand up on their appointed lines,
But all their worth has faded with the sun;
Unchallenged now I cross their strict confines;
The ball is gone, the game is lost and won.

I walk again where once I came to grief,
Crashing to earth, yet holding fast the ball,
Symbol of yet another True Belief,
The last but surely not the least of all:

City Life

To strain and struggle to the end of strength;
To lean on skill, not ask a gift of chance,
To win, or lose, and recognize at length
The game the thing; the rest, a circumstance.

And now the teams are vanished from the field,
But still an echo of their presence clings;
The moon discovers what the day concealed,
The gracefulness and grief of passing things.

Quick as the ball is thrown from hand to hand
And fleetly as the wing three-quarters run,
Swifter shall Time to his defences stand
And bring the fastest falling one by one,

Until the moon, that looked on Stonehenge ground
Before the stones, will rise and sink and set
Above this field, where also will be found
The relics of a mystery men forget.

Politics

Politics

Song of the Squatter

Robert Lowe (1811 - 1892)

The Commissioner bet me a pony — I won;
So he cut off exactly two-thirds of my run;
For he said I was making a fortune too fast,
And profit gained slower the longer would last.

He remarked, as devouring my mutton he sat,
That I suffered my sheep to grow sadly too fat;
That they wasted waste land, did prerogative brown,
And rebelliously nibbled the droits of the Crown

That the creek that divided my station in two
Showed that Nature designed that two fees should be due.
Mr. Riddle assured me 'twas paid but for show;
But he kept it and spent it; that's all that I know.

The Commissioner fined me because I forgot
To return an old ewe that was ill of the rot,
And a poor wry-necked lamb that we kept for a pet:
And he said it was treason such things to forget.

The Commissioner pounded my cattle because
They had mumbled the scrub with their famishing jaws
On the part of the run he had taken away;
And he sold them by auction the costs to defray.

The border police they were out all the day
To look for some thieves who had ransacked my dray,
But the thieves they continued in quiet and peace,
For they'd robbed it themselves had the border police!

Song of the Squatter

When the white thieves had left me the black thieves appeared,
My shepherds they waddied, my cattle they speared;
But for fear of my licence I said not a word,
For I knew it was gone if the Government heard.

The Commissioner's bosom with anger was filled
Against me, because my poor shepherd was killed;
So he straight took away the last third of my run,
And got it transferred to the name of his son.

The son had from Cambridge been lately expelled,
And his licence for preaching most justly withheld!
But this is no cause, the Commissioner says,
Why he should not be fit for my licence to graze.

The cattle that had not been sold at the pound
He took with the run at five shillings all round;
And the sheep the blacks left me at sixpence a head;
"And a very good price!" the Commissioner said.

The Governor told me I justly was served,
That Commissioners never from duty had swerved;
But that if I'd fancy for any more land,
For one pound an acre he'd plenty on land

I'm not very proud; I can dig in a bog,
Feed pigs, or for firewood can split up a log,
Clean shoes, riddle cinders, or help to boil down —
Anything that you please, but graze lands of the Crown!

Politics

The Last of His Tribe

Henry Kendall (1839 - 1882)

He crouches, and buries his face on his knees,
    And hides in the dark of his hair;
For he cannot look up to the storm-smitten trees,
    Or think of the loneliness there —
        Of the loss and the loneliness there.

The wallaroos grope through the tufts of the grass,
    And turn to their coverts for fear;
But he sits in the ashes and lets them pass
    Where the boomerangs sleep with the spear —
        With the nullah, the sling and the spear.

Uloola, behold him! The thunder that breaks
    On the tops of the rocks with the rain,
And the wind which drives up with the salt of the lakes,
    Have made him a hunter again —
        A hunter and fisher again.

For his eyes have been full with a smouldering thought;
    But he dreams of the hunts of yore,
And of foes that he sought, and of fights that he fought
    With those who will battle no more —
        Who will go to the battle no more.

The Last of His Tribe

It is well that the water which tumbles and fills,
    Goes moaning and moaning along;
For an echo rolls out from the sides of the hills,
    And he starts at a wonderful song —
        At the sounds of a wonderful song.

And he sees, through the rents of the scattering fogs,
    The corroboree warlike and grim,
And the lubra who sat by the fire on the logs,
    To watch, like a mourner, for him —
        Like a mother and mourner for him.

Will he go in his sleep from these desolate lands,
    Like a chief, to the rest of his race,
With the honey-voiced woman who beckons, and stands,
    And gleams like a Dream in his face —
        Like a marvellous Dream in his face?

Are You the Cove?

Joseph Furphy (1843 - 1912)

"Are you the Cove?" he spoke the words
As swagmen only can;
The Squatter freezingly inquired,
"What do you mean, my man?"

"Are you the Cove?" his voice was stern,
His look was firm and keen;
Again the Squatter made reply,
"I don't know what you mean."

"O! dash my rags! let's have some sense—
You ain't a fool, by Jove,
Gammon you dunno what I mean;
I mean — are you the Cove?'

'Yes, I'm the Cove," the Squatter said;
The Swagman answered, "Right,
I thought as much: show me some place
Where I can doss tonight."

Second Class Wait Here

Henry Lawson (1867 - 1922)

At suburban railway stations — you may see them as you pass —
There are signboards on the platforms saying "Wait here second class";
And to me the whirr and thunder and the cluck of running gear
Seem to be for ever saying 'Second class wait here —
    "Wait here second class,
    Second class wait here."
Seem to be for ever saying "Second class wait here".

And the second class were waiting in the days of serf and prince,
And the second class are waiting — they've been waiting ever since.
There are gardens in the background, and the line is
    bare and drear,
Yet they wait beneath the signboard sneering "Second class wait here".

I have waited oft in winter, in the mornings dark and damp,
When the ashphalt platform glistened underneath the lonely lamp.
Glistened on the brick-faced cutting "Sellum's Soap" and
    "Blower's Beer".
Glistened on the enamelled signboards with their "Second class wait here".

And the others seemed like burglars, slouched and muffled
    to the throats,
Standing round apart and silent in their shoddy overcoats,

Politics

And the wind among the wires, and the poplars bleak and bare,
Seemed to be for ever snarling, snarling "Second class wait here".

Out beyond the further suburb, 'neath a chimney-stack alone
Lay the works of Grinder brothers, with a platform of their own;
And I waited there and suffered, waited there for many a day,
Slaved beneath a phantom signboard, telling our class to wait here.

Ah! a man must feel revengeful for a boyhood such as mine,
God! I hate the very houses near the workshop by the line;
And the smell of railway stations, and the roar of running gear,
And the scornful-seeming signboards, saying "Second class wait here".

There's a train, with Death for driver, that is ever going past;
And there are no class compartments, and we all must go at last
For the long white jasper platform with an Eden in the rear;
And there won't be any signboards, saying "Second class wait here".

Freedom on the Wallaby

Henry Lawson (1867 - 1922)

Australia's a big country
    An' Freedom's humping bluey,
An' Freedom's on the wallaby
    Oh! don't you hear 'er cooey?
She's just begun to boomerang,
    She'll knock the tyrants silly,
She's goin' to light another fire
    And boil another billy.

Our fathers toiled for bitter bread
    While loafers thrived beside 'em,
But food to eat and clothes to wear,
    Their native land denied 'em.
An' so they left their native land
    In spite of their devotion,
An' so they came, or if they stole,
    Were sent across the ocean.

Then Freedom couldn't stand the glare
    O' Royalty's regalia,
She left the loafers where they were,
    An' came out to Australia.
But now across the mighty main
    The chains have come ter bind her —
She little thought to see again
    The wrongs she left behind her.

Politics

Our parents toil'd to make a home —
    Hard grubbin 'twas an' clearin' —
They wasn't crowded much with lords
    When they was pioneering.
But now that we have made the land
    A garden full of promise,
Old Greed must crook 'is dirty hand
    And come ter take it from us.

So we must fly a rebel flag,
    As others did before us,
And we must sing a rebel song
    And join in rebel chorus.
We'll make the tyrants feel the sting
    O' those that they would throttle;
They needn't say the fault is ours
    If blood should stain the wattle!

Faces in the Street

Henry Lawson (1867 - 1922)

They lie, the men who tell us in a loud decisive tone
That want is here a stranger, and that misery's unknown;
For where the nearest suburb and the city proper meet
My window-sill is level with the faces in the street —
     Drifting past, drifting past,
     To the beat of weary feet —
While I sorrow for the owners of those faces in the street.

And cause I have to sorrow, in a land so young and fair,
To see upon those faces stamped the marks of Want and Care;
I look in vain for traces of the fresh and fair and sweet
In sallow, sunken faces that are drifting through the street —
     Drifting on, drifting on,
     To the scrape of restless feet;
I can sorrow for the owners of the faces in the street.

In hours before the dawning dims the starlight in the sky
The wan and weary faces first begin to trickle by,
Increasing as the moments hurry on with morning feet,
Till like a pallid river flow the faces in the street —
     Flowing in, flowing in,
     To the beat of hurried feet —
Ah! I sorrow for the owners of those faces in the street.

The human river dwindles when 'tis past the hour of eight,
Its waves go flowing faster in the fear of being late;
But slowly drag the moments, whilst beneath the dust and heat
The city grinds the owners of the faces in the street —
     Grinding body, grinding soul,
     Yielding scarce enough to eat —
Oh! I sorrow for the owners of the faces in the street.

And then the only faces till the sun is sinking down
Are those of outside toilers and the idlers of the town,
Save here and there a face that seems a stranger in the street,
Tells of the city's unemployed upon his weary beat —
    Drifting round, drifting round,
    To the tread of listless feet —
Ah! My heart aches for the owner of that sad face in the street.

And when the hours on lagging feet have slowly dragged away,
And sickly yellow gaslights rise to mock the going day,
Then flowing past my window like a tide in its retreat,
Again I see the pallid stream of faces in the street —
    Ebbing out, ebbing out,
    To the drag of tired feet,
While my heart is aching dumbly for the faces in the street.

And now all blurred and smirched with vice the day's
    sad pages end,
For while the short "large hours" toward the longer
    "small hours" trend,
With smiles that mock the wearer, and with words
    that half entreat,
Delilah pleads for custom at the corner of the street —
    Sinking down, sinking down,
    Battered wreck by tempests beat —
A dreadful, thankless trade is hers, that Woman of the Street.

Faces in the Street

But, ah! to dreader things than these our fair young city comes,
For in its heart are growing thick the filthy dens and slums,
Where human forms shall rot away in sties for swine unmeet,
And ghostly faces shall be seen unfit for any street —
    Rotting out, rotting out,
    For the lack of air and meat —
In dens of vice and horror that are hidden from the street.

I wonder would the apathy of wealthy men endure
Were all their windows level with the faces of the Poor?
Ah! Mammon's slaves, your knees shall knock, your hearts
    in terror beat,
When God demands a reason for the sorrows of the street,
    The wrong things and the bad things
    And the sad things that we meet
In the filthy lane and alley, and the cruel, heartless street.

I left the dreadful corner where the steps are never still,
And sought another window overlooking gorge and hill;
But when the night came dreary with the driving rain and sleet,
They haunted me — the shadows of those faces in the street,
    Flitting by, flitting by,
    Flitting by with noiseless feet,
And with cheeks but little paler than the real ones in the street.

Politics

Once I cried: "Oh, God Almighty! if Thy might doth still endure,
Now show me in a vision for the wrongs of Earth a cure."
And, lo! with shops all shuttered I beheld a city's street,
And in the warning distance heard the tramp of many feet,
    Coming near, coming near,
    To a drum's dull distant beat,
And soon I saw the army that was marching down the street.

Then, like a swollen river that has broken bank and wall,
The human flood came pouring with the red flags over all,
And kindled eyes all blazing bright with revolution's heat,
And flashing swords reflecting rigid faces in the street.
    Pouring on, pouring on,
    To a drum's loud threatening beat,
And the war-hymns and the cheering of the people in the street.

And so it must be while the world goes rolling round its course,
The warning pen shall write in vain, the warning voice grow hoarse,
But not until a city feels Red Revolution's feet
Shall its sad people miss awhile the terrors of the street —
    The dreadful everlasting strife
    For scarcely clothes and meat
In that pent track of living death — the city's cruel street.

Waltzing Matilda

A.B. "Banjo" Paterson (1864 - 1941)

Oh there once was a swagman camped in the billabongs,
    Under the shade of a Coolibah tree;
And he sang as he looked at the old billy boiling
    "Who'll come a-waltzing Matilda with me."

Who'll come a-waltzing Matilda, my darling.
    Who'll come a-waltzing Matilda with me.
Waltzing Matilda and leading a water-bag.
    Who'll come a-waltzing Matilda with me.

Up came the jumbuck to drink at the waterhole,
    Up jumped the swagman and grabbed him with glee;
And he sang as he put him away in his tucker-bag,
    "You'll come a-waltzing Matilda with me."

Who'll come a-waltzing Matilda, my darling.
    Who'll come a-waltzing Matilda with me.
Waltzing Matilda and leading a water-bag.
    Who'll come a-waltzing Matilda with me.

Politics

Up came the squatter a-riding his thoroughbred;
    Up came policemen — one, two, and three.
"Whose is the jumbuck you've got in the tucker-bag?
    You'll come a-waltzing Matilda with we."

Who'll come a-waltzing Matilda, my darling.
    Who'll come a-waltzing Matilda with me.
Waltzing Matilda and leading a water-bag.
    Who'll come a-waltzing Matilda with me.

Up sprang the swagman and jumped in the waterhole,
    Drowning himself by the Coolibah tree;
And his voice can be heard as it sings in the billabongs,
    "Who'll come a-waltzing Matilda with me."

Who'll come a-waltzing Matilda, my darling.
    Who'll come a-waltzing Matilda with me.
Waltzing Matilda and leading a water-bag.
    Who'll come a-waltzing Matilda with me.

This is the original version of "Waltzing Matilda", as written by 'Banjo' Paterson in 1895. In 1903 it was printed as sheet music with altered words in the version we are all familiar with.

Tall Hat

Victor Daley (1858 - 1905)

Who rules the world with iron rod? —
    The person in the Tall Silk Hat.
He is its sordid lord and god —
    Self-centred in a Shrine of Fat.

He keeps the Hoi Polloi in peace,
    With opiates of Kingdom Come:
His is the Glory that is Grease,
    The Grandeur that is Rum.

He sends the nations forth to fight,
    The war-ships grim across the foam:
They battle for the right — *his* right —
    A mortgage over hearth and home.

He strokes his stomach with a hand
    Bejewelled, and he scorns the poor;
"One thing," he says, "they understand —
    Bouche va toujours—toujours, toujours.

"The workman strikes—and starves, and dies:
    His widow on his doorstep begs;
I hear his children's bitter cries —
    And calmly eat my ham-and-eggs."

Let us, who are by Fate forbid
    To live in rich, luxurious ease,
Thank fate, or kindly God, who did
    Not make us like these Pharisees.

The Glorious Future

from 'Australasia'
William Charles Wentworth (1793 - 1872)

Celestial poesy! whose genial sway
Earth's farthest habitable shores obey;
Whose inspirations shed their sacred light
Far as the regions of the Arctic night,
And to the Laplander his Boreal gleam
Endear not less than Phoebus' brighter beam —
Descend thou also on my native land,
And on some mountain summit take thy stand;
Thence issuing soon a purer fount be seen
Than charm'd Castalia or fam'd Hippocrene;
And there a richer, nobler fame arise
Than on Parnassus met th' adoring eyes.
And tho', bright goddess, on those far blue hills,
That pour their thousand swift pellucid rills,
Where Warragamba's rage has rent in twain
Opposing mountains, thund'ring to the plain,
No child of song has yet invoked thy aid,
'Neath their primaeval solitary shade, —
Still, gracious pow'r, some kindling soul inspire
To wake to life my country's unknown lyre,
That from creation's date has slumb'ring lain,
Or only breath'd some savage uncouth strain, —
And grant that yet an Austral Milton's song
Pactolus-like flow deep and rich along, —
An Austral Shakespeare rise, whose living page
To Nature true may charm in ev'ry age; —
And that an Austral Pinder daring soar,
Where not the Theban Eagle reach'd before.

from 'Australasia'

And, O Britannia! shouldst thou cease to ride
Despotic Empress of old Ocean's tide; —
Should thy tam'd Lion—spent his former might —
No longer roar the terror of the fight; —
Should e'er arrive that dark disastrous hour,
When, bow'd by luxury, thou yield'st to power; —
When thou, no longer freest of the free,
To some proud victor bend'st the vanquished knee; —
May all thy glories in another sphere
Relume, and shine more brightly still than here;
May this—thy last-born infant—then arise,
To glad thy heart, and greet thy parent eyes;
And Australasia float, with flag unfurl'd,
A new Britannia in another world!

Colonial Nomenclature
John Dunmore Lang (1799 - 1878)

'Twas said of Greece two thousand years ago,
    That every stone i' the land had got a name.
Of New South Wales too, men will soon say so too;
    But every stone there seems to get the same.
"Macquarie" for a name is all *the go*:
    The old Scotch Governor was fond of fame.
Macquarie Street, Place, Port, Fort ,Town, Lake, River:
"Lachlan Macquarie, Esquire, Governor", for ever!

I like the native names, as Parramatta,
    And Illawarra, and Woolloomoolloo;
Nandowra, Woongarora, Bulkomatta,
    Tomah, Toongabbie, Mittagong, Meroo;
Buckobble, Cumleroy, and Coolingatta.
    The Warragumby, Bargo, Burradoo;
Cookbundoon, Carrabaiga, Wingecarribbee,
The Wollondilly, Yurumbon, Bungarribbee.

I hate your Goulburn Downs and Goulburn Plains,
    And Goulburn River and the Goulburn Range,
And Mount Goulburn and Goulburn Vale! One's brains
    Are turned with Goulburns! Vile scorbutic mange
For immortality! Had I the reigns
    Of Government a fortnight, I would change
These Downing Street appellatives, and give
The country names that should deserve to live.

I'd have Mount Hampden and Mount Marvell, and
    Mount Wallace and Mount Bruce at the old Bay.
I'd have them all the highest in the land,
    That men might see them twenty leagues away.
I'd have the Plains of Marathon beyond
    Some mountain pass yclept Thermopylae.
Such are th' immortal names that should be written
On all thy new discoveries, Great Britain!

Yes! let some badge of liberty appear
    On every mountain and on every plain
Where Britain's power is known, or far or near,
    That freedom there may have an endless reign!
Then though she die, in some revolving year,
    A race may rise to make her live again!
The future slave may lisp the patriot's name
And his breast kindle with a kindred flame!

The Australian Sunrise
James Cuthbertson (1851 - 1910)

The Morning Star paled slowly, the Cross hung low to the sea,
And down the shadowy reaches the tide came swirling free,
The lustrous purple blackness of the soft Australian night
Waned in the gray awakening that heralded the light;
Out of the dying darkness over the forest dim
The pearly dew of the dawning clung to each giant limb,
Till the sun came up from ocean, red with the cold sea mist,
And smote on the limestone ridges, and the shining
        tree-tops kissed;
Then the fiery Scorpion vanished, the magpie's note was heard,
And the wind in the she-oak wavered, and the
        honeysuckles stirred,
The airy golden vapour rose from the river breast,
The kingfisher came darting out of his crannied nest,
And the bulrushes and reed-beds put off their sallow gray
And burnt with cloudy crimson at dawning of the day.

Our Coming Countrymen
Henry Parkes (1815 - 1906)

England's poor who wanderers be
On her highway o'er the sea!
Trodden long in England's dust —
Out at last from England thrust!

Children of the former brave,
Who, on the battle-field and wave,
Fought for England in the time,
Ere her poverty was crime.

Ye, whose labour and whose skill,
And whose scorn of every ill,
Save the woe ordain'd by state,
Made her greatest of the great! —

Whose intelligence and power,
(Though ye be old England's poor,)
Best support her mighty name
Of imperishable fame.

Ye who come — when statesmen say
That is left the only way
To appease lean Hunger's cries —
Out to England's colonies.

Know ye what fair masters wait —
Master both and magistrate —
Ye to give your sweat for bread,
When Australia's shores ye tread.

The Glorious Future

Know ye, gentlemen are they,
Who in open daylight say
England's convicts they prefer
To you pauper-scum from her! —

Convicts, for they cheaper are,
And more governable far;
Convicts, with no idle child
To be ration'd in the wild! —

In the wild, where go ye must,
And to these men's mercies trust;
And, arise what quarrels may,
Their adjudgement still obey! —

Where revenge and lust ne'er sleep,
Let wild nature smile or weep,
Unabash'd as unforgiven,
When the sun looks down from Heaven!

Where all British law is dead,
As our senators have said,
And the honest pay a price
For the sufferance of vice.

"Ample room for life" is there,
And it is a region fair, —
Ample room, but not for man
In the heaven-appointed plan.

Where the cedars fringe the river
In the summer light for ever,
And the plain and valley pine
For the plough and harrows tine;

Not a single cottager,
Like the men your fathers were,
Is there through the sun-bright regions;
Only sheep in countless legions.

One man's flocks, for you to tend,
O'er a kingdom's space extend, —
You or isle-barbarian,
China's slave or cheaper man.

Though the factory's crowded floor
Hold you not as heretofore;
Though ye tread the fragrant ground,
With the free pure air all around;

Though no workhouse mandate now
May your suffering spirits bow;
Though ye feel, and justly may,
Ye have won your bread each day:

Ye all Christian faith will need,
Not to curse your lot indeed,
Still pursued by wretchedness,
New and different, but not less.

The Glorious Future

The Australian

Arthur Adams (1872 - 1936)

Once more this autumn-earth is ripe,
Parturient of another type.

While with the Past old nations merge
His foot is on the Future's verge.

They watch him, as they huddle, pent,
Striding a spacious continent,

Above the level desert's marge
Looming in his aloofness large.

No flower with fragile sweetness graced–
A lank weed wrestling with the waste;

Pallid of face and gaunt of limb,
The sweetness withered out of him;

Sombre, indomitable, wan,
The juices dried, the glad youth gone.

A little weary from his birth,
His laugh the spectre of a mirth,

Bitter beneath a bitter sky,
To Nature he has no reply.

Wanton, perhaps, and cruel. Yes,
Is not his sun more merciless?

So drab and neutral is his day,
He finds a splendour in the grey,

And from his life's monotony
He draws a dreary melody.

When earth so poor a banquet makes
His pleasures at a gulp he takes;

The feast is his to the last crumb:
Drink while he can...the drought will come.

His heart a sudden tropic flower,
He loves and loathes within an hour.

Yet you who by the pools abide,
Judge not the man who swerves aside;

He sees beyond your hazy fears;
He roads the desert of the years;

Rearing his cities in the sand,
He builds where even God has banned;

The Glorious Future

With green a continent he crowns,
And stars a wilderness with towns;

With paths the distances he snares;
His gyves of steel the great plain wears.

A child who takes a world for toy,
To build a nation or destroy,

His childish features frozen stern,
His manhood's task he has to learn –

From feeble tribes to federate
One white and peace-encompassed State.

But if there be no goal to reach?
The track lies open, dawns beseech!

Enough that he lay down his load
A little farther on the road.

So, toward undreamt-of-destinies
He slouches down the centuries.

The Song of Australia
Caroline Carleton (1820 - 1874)

There is a land where summer skies
Are gleaming with a thousand dyes,
Blending in witching harmonies;
And grassy knoll, and forest height,
Is flushing in the rosy light,
And all above is azure bright —
Australia!

There is a land where honey flows,
Where laughing corn luxuriant grows,
Land of the myrtle and the rose,
On hill and plain the clust'ring vine,
Is gushing out with purple wine,
And cups are quaffed to thee and thine —
Australia!

There is a land where treasures shine
Deep in the dark unfathom'd mine,
For worshippers at Mammon's shrine,
Where gold lies hid, and rubies gleam,
And fabled wealth no more doth seem
The idle fancy of a dream —
Australia!

The Glorious Future

There is a land where homesteads peep
From sunny plain and woodland steep,
And love and joy bright vigils keep,
Where the glad voice of childish glee
Is mingling with the melody
Of nature's hidden minstrelsy —
                    Australia!

There is a land where floating free,
From mountain top to girdling sea,
A proud flag waves exultingly,
And Freedom's sons the banner bear,
No shackl'd slave can breathe the air,
Fairest of Britain's daughters fair —
                    Australia!

Index

Titles and authors

11.11.1918 125

A Bush Christening 27
A Convict's Lament on the Death of Captain Logan 53
A Gallop of Fire 85
A Gray and Dusty Daylight Flows 98
A Hot Day in Sydney 68
A Midsummer Noon in the Australian Forest 81
Adams, Arthur 174
Are You the Cove? 152
'Australasia' 166

Because She Would Ask Me Why I Loved Her 97
Bell-Birds 78
Boake, Barcroft 109
Botany Bay Courtship 57
Brennan, Christopher John 97, 98, 99, 143
Bruce, Robert 106
Butchered to Make a Dutchman's Holiday 121

Carleton, Caroline 177
Christmas Day near Lake Torrens, 1864 106
Clancy of the Overflow 38
Colonial Experience 55
Colonial Nomenclature 168
Cuthbertson, James 170

Daley, Victor 141, 163
Dawn and Sunrise in the Snowy Mountains 80
Dennis, C.J. 130, 134, 137

'E', (Mary Fullerton) 49, 96
Echoes of Wheels... 47
Emus 96
Essex Evans, George 18, 114
Esson, Louis 113

Faces in the Street 157
Fairbridge, Wolfe 91
Field, Barron 66

Fire in the Heavens 99
Football Field: Evening 145
Foott, Mary Hannay 75
Freedom on the Wallaby 155
Furphy, Joseph 152

Goodge, W.T. 17
Gordon, Adam Lindsay 14

Harpur, Charles 80, 81

Jim Jones at Botany Bay 52
Jim's Whip 111

Kendall, Henry 76, 78, 150

Lang, John Dunmore 168
Lawson, Henry 43, 117, 153, 155, 157
Lowe, Robert 148

Mackellar, Dorothea 89
Manning, Frederic 123
Maurice, Furnley (Frank Wilmot) 46, 47
McCarthy's Brew: a Gulf Country Yarn 18
McKellar, J. A. R. 125, 145
Middleton's Rouseabout 116
Morant, Harry ("Breaker") 20, 119, 121
Mulga Bill's Bicycle 25
My Country 89

Native Companions Dancing 102
Neilson, John Shaw 87, 100, 101, 102, 103

O'Brien, John 33
On the Derwent 86
Our Coming Countrymen 171

Parkes, Henry 171
Past Carin' 117
Paterson, A.B. "Banjo" 23, 25, 27, 29, 38, 40, 128, 161
Penn-Smith, Frank 86
Pitt, Marie E. J. 83, 85

Return 49

Said Hanrahan 33
Second Class Wait Here 153
Since the Country Carried Sheep 119
Song Be Delicate 101
Song of the Shingle-Splitters 76
Song of the Squatter 148

Tall Hat 163
The Australian 174
The Australian Sunrise 170
The Banks of the Condamine 94
The Banksia 91
The Call of Stoush 130
The Diggins-Oh 62
The Geebung Polo Club 23
The Great Australian Adjective 17
The Kangaroo 66
The Last of His Tribe 150
The Man from Ironbark 128
The Man from Snowy River 29
The Maranoa Drovers 61
The Old Australian Ways 40
The Orange Tree 103
The Play 137
The Poor, Poor Country 87
The Sick Stockrider 14
The Shearer's Wife 113
The Smoker Parrot 100
The Song of Australia 177
The Song of Old Joe Swallow 43
The Trenches 123
The West Coasters (Tasmania) 83
The Wild Colonial Boy 59
The Woman at the Washtub 141
The Women of the West 114
The Yellow Gas 143
They've Builded... 46

Waltzing Matilda 161
Washing Day 134
Wentworth, William Charles 166
Where the Dead Men Lie 109
Where the Pelican Builds 75
Who's Riding Old Harlequin Now? 20

First lines

A few thin strips of fleecy clouds lie long	80
A gray and dusty daylight flows	98
All you on emigration bent	72
"Are you the Cove?" he spoke the words	152
At suburban railway stations — you may see them as you pass —	153
Australia sings her Over-land	83
Australia's a big country	155
Before the glare o' dawn I rise	113
But here, no merry bells you hear	106
By channels of coolness, the echoes are calling	78
Celestial poesy! whose genial sway	166
Cross bars and posts, the echo of distant bells	145
Echoes of wheels and singing lashes	47
Endless lanes sunken in the clay	123
England's poor who wanderers be	171
Fire in the heavens, and fire along the hills	99
He crouches, and buries his face on his knees	150
He has the full moon on his breast	100
Hold hard, Ned! Lift me down once more, and lay me in the shade.	14
I am a native of the land of Erin	53
I had written him a letter which I had, for want of better	38
I've come back all skin and bone	62
If questioning could make us wise	97
In prison cell I sadly sit	121
In the dark wild wood, where the lone owl broods	76
It was somewhere up the country in a land of rock and scrub	23
It was the man from Ironbark who struck the Sydney town	128
Kangaroo, Kangaroo!	66
Let your song be delicate	101
My annals have it so	96
Not a bird disturbs the air	81

Now and up and down the sidling brown	117
O this weather! this weather!	68
O, listen for a moment lads, and hear me tell my tale —	52
Oh, 'twas a poor country, in Autumn it was bare	87
Oh, hark the dogs are barking, love	94
On the blue plains in wintry days	102
On the outer Barcoo where the churches are few	27
Once a jolly swagman camped by a billabong	161
Once more this autumn-earth is ripe	174
Out on the wastes of the Never Never	109
Pale the evening falls	86
The Commissioner bet me a pony — I won	148
The Currency Lads may fill their glasses	57
The horses were ready, the rails were down	75
The little gipsy vi'lits, they wus peepin' thro' the green	134
The London lights are far abeam	40
The love of field and coppice	89
The Morning Star paled slowly, the Cross hung low to the sea	170
The night is dark and stormy, and the sky is clouded o'er	61
The ruthless bush is grown along the track	49
The spear blades of the Xamia are erect	91
The sunburnt —— stockman stood	17
The yellow gas is fired from street to street	143
The young girl stood beside me.	103
Tall and freckled and sandy	116
The teams of Black McCarthy crawled adown the Norman road	18
The Woman at the Washtub	141
There is a land where summer skies	177
There was movement at the station, for the word has passed around	29
They are mustering cattle on Brigalow Vale	20
They left the vine-wreathed cottage and the mansion on the hill	114

186

They lie, the men who tell us in a loud decisive tone	157
They're bones in full battalions now	125
They've builded wooden timber tracks	46
'Tis of a wild Colonial Boy, Jack Doolan was his name	59
'Twas Mulga Bill, from Eaglehawk, that caught the cycling craze	25
'Twas said of Greece two thousand years ago	168
We trucked the cows to Homebush, saw the girls, and started back	119
"We'll all be rooned," said Hanrahan	33
When first I came to Sydney Cove	171
When I was up the country in the rough and early days,	43
When the north wind moans thro' the blind creek courses	85
"Wot's in a name?" she sez...And then she sighs	137
Who rules the world with iron rod? —	161
Wot price ole Ginger Mick? 'E's done a break —	130
Yes, there it hangs upon the wall	111

187

Acknowledgements

Poetry

"My Country", by Dorothea Mackellar, by arrangement with the
    copyright owner, The Estate of Dorothea Mackellar,
    c/- Curtis Brown (Aust) Pty Ltd

"Said Hanrahan", by John O'Brien, from *Around The Boree Log*,
    c/- Harper Collins Publishers Australia.

Cover Artwork

Frederick McCubbin
Landscape, 1914
Oil on Canvas, 91.5 x 55.9cm
Art Gallery of New South Wales
Photo: AGNSW